DECORATING WITH FABRIC

DECORATING WITH

FABRIC

Hundreds of Exciting and Creative Fabric Ideas for
Decorating Your Home Quickly and Inexpensively

by Judy Lindahl

Butterick Publishing

PICTURE CREDITS

Color Section 1
First page: Copyright © Butterick Publishing.   Second page: Waverly Fabrics, A Division of F. Schumacher & Co., "Flora Danica".   Third page: Waverly Fabrics, A Division of F. Schumacher & Co., "Jewel Flowers".   Fourth page: Top—Copyright © Butterick Publishing. Bottom left—Butterick Archives. Bottom right—Butterick Archives.

Color Section 2
Photographs by Edward Scibetta. Arrangements by Charles Laemmle for Abraham & Straus, Brooklyn, New York, and Brooke Worden Rosenfeld of Posh Parties, Inc. Settings courtesy of Joseph Genty.

Color Section 3
First page: Butterick Archives. Second page: Top—Bloomcraft Inc., "Sea Isle". Bottom—Bloomcraft Inc., "Jack" (round cloth) and "Merrill" (table topper). Third page: Top—Photograph by Edward Scibetta. Arrangement by Charles Laemmle for Abraham & Straus, Brooklyn, New York. Bottom—Bloomcraft Inc., "Beaulieu".   Fourth page: Photographs by Edward Scibetta. Chair re-covering by Charles Laemmle.

Printed in the United States of America
Book design by Bobye G. List
Illustrations by Phoebe A. Gaughan

To my mother, and to my husband Buzz for his patience and understanding.

CONTENTS

AN INTRODUCTION TO FABRIC DECORATING

Decorating with fabric is for everyone—men and women, home-owners and apartment dwellers. It is one of the best ways to get the maximum effect for the amount of time and money invested. And you don't have to be a professional or an expert to get excellent results. You can cover anything, from the smallest desk accessory to walls, ceilings, furnishings, and floors. The most important assets you can bring to it are your own optimism, desire, and imagination. Your confidence and expertise will increase as you move from project to project. There is nothing quite like the feeling of satisfaction you'll get as you watch walls, windows, accessories, and furnishings come alive with the color, pattern, and texture of fabric using the skill of your own workmanship.

Fabric is without doubt the most flexible decorating medium available to you. If you don't sew, you can staple. If you can't staple, try fusing, or starching, or gluing. There are so many techniques and combinations of techniques to use that you can cover any surface you want with fabric. And what other medium can be draped, gathered, pleated, stiffened, padded, quilted, stuffed, and smoothed into place? Fabric also can conceal flaws or imperfections in workmanship or in the object itself. Often, you will need to do little if anything to prepare the surface to be covered. And on top of all that, fabric has the economical advantage of being retrievable, or as temporary as you want it to be. After you've enjoyed your fabric-covered walls or that spectacular wall hanging, you can remove the fabric and turn it into other projects—quilts, patchwork, pillows, or placemats, to name a few. If you're renting, your fabric can move with you. So why wait? Start planning your first projects right now.

HOW TO BEGIN

Selecting a Fabric

Evaluate any fabric you are thinking of using for decorating by asking yourself questions such as, "What am I asking of this fabric? How much use and abuse must it take? Do I just want to look at it—as in wall hangings, on screens or walls? Or must it withstand abrasion—as on tables or floors? Will it be subjected to sunlight? What kind and frequency of cleaning will it need to withstand?" By looking at where you are putting the fabric, what you expect of it, and what you can anticipate because of the actual construction, fiber content, finish, and so on, you will guide yourself to a wise fabric choice. Be careful, but don't restrict yourself with preconceived notions. Be open to new ideas and fabrics you can use in unusual ways and in imaginative combinations.

An important test you can make with any fabric is to drape several feet of it and step back in order to view it from the same perspective as you would in the room. It is best to see the fabric in the location it is to go; color, design, and texture can be assessed more easily under the actual lighting and scale of the room where it is to be used. If this is not possible, make a small notebook of textile swatches already in the room. When you go shopping take this with you so you can compare colors and textures before selecting a fabric. For small projects drape the fabric over or around the object to check for scale and centering of the design.

Another test is to gather and drape fabrics that will be handled in that manner—for draperies, curtains, shirred walls, or lampshades. Gathering or pleating can change the look of a design because of the way it breaks up the pattern and the way light reflects on its texture. Gathering or pleating can make some designs more acceptable to the eye and are good ways to introduce a texture change in a room, making the all-over use of one fabric pleasing by adding depth to the flat look of the fabric application. Of course, some fabrics and designs may be more attractive used flat, for roller shades, Roman shades, or walls, for example, where the full impact of the design is obvious. Evaluate each fabric both ways, and perhaps combine the two effects.

Fabric is all around us. You need not restrict yourself to decorator fabrics, specifically designed and manufactured for use in decorating, although they do have definite advantages built in. For example, such fabrics are usually 48 to 60 inches wide, firmly woven, often stain and wrinkle resistant, and come in a wide range of weights and textures. Best of all, they have a pattern match near the selvage for economy and ease of matching. Other fabrics may not have all these benefits, but the more there are, the easier your work will be.

Today's handsome decorator sheets with their variety of patterns are a natural for decorating, too. Their width makes them a good choice for tablecloths, drapes, wall coverings, and so on. Their weight may make them unsatisfactory for drapes in very humid climates since moist air can make them rather limp. They are fine for shorter, fuller curtains, however. You should consider the amount of use sheet fabrics will have to take before using them for slipcovers or on objects that receive lots of wear. Also, look for the location of the pattern match—if it is not near the edge of the sheets, the result will be a loss of fabric on every sheet used. But over all, sheets are an extremely economical source of well-designed fabric. Remember that sheets can be used as the fabric in almost all the projects suggested in this book.

Refer to the following chart of sheet sizes before hemming when planning your decorating projects.

Flat Sheet Size	Approx. Yardage in			Attached Hem (Separate)*	Self Hem (Turned Under)
	36''	45''	58'' fabric		
Twin	5	4	3⅛	66'' x 94''	66'' x 104''
Full (Double)	6	4¾	3⅞	81'' x 94''	81'' x 104''
Queen	7	5⅞	4½	90'' x 100''	90'' x 110''
King	8¾	7	5⅜	108'' x 100''	108'' x 110''

Fitted Sheets**	Mattress Size
Twin	39'' x 75''
Full (Double)	54'' x 75''
Queen	60'' x 80''
King	72'' x 84''

*Save the hems when removed from sheets of this type. The strips can be used in many ways, especially as ruffles on curtains, tablecloths, pillows, and so on.

**If seams are let out on the four corners, this allows an additional 8 or 9 inches on each side of the sheet.

In choosing fabric, resist thinking only in terms of woven fabric. Knits are gaining increasing acceptance for everything from slipcovers to wall coverings, bedspreads to draperies. Because they "give and recover" so well knits are ideal for wrapped projects such as chair seats, folding screens, and storage boxes. Because they shed wrinkles and drape beautifully, they are superb in draperies and curtains. The knit you choose, however, should be appropriate for the individual project. Vinyls and fake furs are specialty fabrics that should also be considered. They require careful handling, but are worth the effort for the special effects they give.

When you work with woven fabrics you will need to consider the grainline and the way the design is printed in relation to it. The grainline is the way in which the lengthwise and crosswise threads lie in relation to each other. Ideally, fabrics should be as nearly on grain as possible, with lengthwise and crosswise threads forming right (90°) angles to each other. This is especially important when selecting fabrics for projects such as drapes, curtains, stapled walls, and dipped roller shades. If the fabric is not on grain it will not hang properly.

ON GRAIN

OFF GRAIN (BIAS)

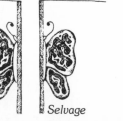

OFF GRAIN (BOW)

To check the grain of a fabric, pull or follow a thread all the way across from selvage to selvage. Cut the fabric along that thread. If the lengthwise and crosswise threads are not at right angles to each other, the fabric is off grain. Sometimes you will be able to straighten the threads by pulling them in the opposite direction on the short ends, as indicated by the arrows in the illustrations. Some fabrics cannot be straightened because the threads are locked in place in manufacturing by applied surface treatments and finishes.

Next, look at the printed design in relation to the grainline. Fabrics may be printed on or off grain, too. To look its best, a printed design must be placed straight. A crooked grain can cause the fabric to pull or draw to one side. When the fabric is bonded or glued, often you can follow the design and not be too concerned with the grain. But a fabric that is very off grain will cause nothing but problems. The best solution is to examine the fabric carefully before you buy.

ADDITIONAL GUIDELINES TO FABRIC SELECTION AND HANDLING

- Firmly woven or knitted fabrics are the easiest to work with and the most durable.
- All-over prints are easiest to apply. They tend to keep your eyes moving and conceal imperfections in the object and workmanship. If the design is small it may not require matching.
- Fabrics with all-over patterns or darker backgrounds will show soiling less quickly than light colored, open-ground prints.
- Decorator fabrics always have a pattern match near the selvages. This results in a better flow of design and less waste of fabric.
- In every patterned fabric a design motif will be repeated at regular intervals; this is called the design repeat. Check the distance between the design repeat. The larger the repeat is, the more fabric is required for matching. Repeats average 12 to 24 inches on most fabrics.

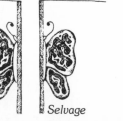

A   *Selvage*

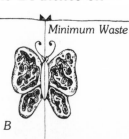

Minimum Waste

B

• *Note:* This is one of the most frequently overlooked factors in figuring fabric yardage, and it can be a critical one. It is always a good idea to buy a little extra yardage. It need never go to waste. There are so many delightful accessories that are easily made that you'll always be able to put the extra fabric to good use.

• Generally the design will be either a straight match, with the repeating motif appearing straight across at the selvages, or a drop match, where the repeating motifs are staggered at the selvages and the fabric must be dropped in order to match them. The drop match is a visual trick to make the design seem larger. It is most often used on relatively narrow fabrics.

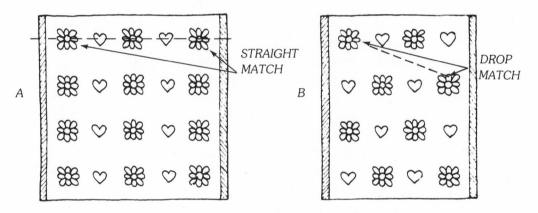

• Using wider fabrics means fewer seams, an advantage for such projects as bedspreads, drapes, tablecloths, and slipcovers.

• Clipping or removing the selvage often permits a stretchy, lengthwise grain to hang more evenly without puckers (especially on drapes or stapled wall treatments).

• Fabrics must be able to withstand moisture if glue, paste, or starch will be used.

• It is wise to preshrink the fabric only if it will need to be washed later, or if a test sample indicates a greater than desirable amount of shrinkage. The latter would be important for projects where fabric would be pasted down with butted seams that could shrink apart as the fabric dried. Otherwise it is better not to wash the fabric, since the finishes on new fabrics help them stay crisp and clean longer. Once laundered, they soil sooner and more easily.

• If the fabric will be used near a light source, as at windows or for lampshades, be sure to check for the way the light is diffused and the way the fabric appears with light behind it.

In summary, just thinking the project through is the best way to be sure of making a good choice of fabric. The more you do, the more you learn, the easier it becomes, and the more confidence you gain.

Selecting a Technique

How should you attach the fabric, once you've chosen it, to whatever it is you're decorating? Should you sew, staple, fuse, glue, starch, or use spray glue? Obviously, with so many techniques for applying fabric, the one or ones you choose will be influenced by:

- The fabric itself
- What tools or materials you have on hand or are available
- How comfortable you are with various tools and methods
- The surface to be covered
- How much time it will take
- What will be most durable or most temporary, as desired.

For example, to cover a wood Parsons table, you might sew a fitted slipcover, wrap and staple the fabric, glue the fabric, starch the fabric, or fuse the fabric. On the other hand a plastic Parsons table could be glued, starched, or slipcovered, but not fused or stapled. Not every project can be handled in so many ways, but it is important to recognize that you do have choices. I am happiest when I combine several techniques to achieve professional results quickly and easily. As you acquaint yourself with a variety of methods, you will automatically do the same.

In the chapters that follow often it will be necessary to illustrate only one method or technique for a project. But if other methods are suggested, think them through and then decide which is best for you—which you feel comfortable with, which works for you, and which will produce the result you really want.

THE CHOICES

- Sewing
- Stapling
- Liquid Starch
- Fusible Webs
- Spray Glues
- White or Craft Glues
- Wallpaper Paste

SEWING

Sewing by machine or by hand is obviously a foundation for many projects, but not knowing how to sew is not a deterrent to decorating with fabric. You will simply become more creative at combining other techniques to achieve a desired goal.

Plain Seams

Most seams in decorating are standard, as for other sewing, but they are usually ½ inch deep instead of the ⅝ inch used in clothing. If seam allowances are enclosed within a project—as in pillows, lined drapes, or curtains—they are rarely finished, as excessive finishing can cause puckering. Selvages are often trimmed off before sewing and measuring. If you do include them in a seam it may be necessary to clip them every few inches to reduce the chances of puckering.

French Seams

French seams are used a great deal for sheer fabrics, especially in window treatments and other projects where exposed raw edges are undesirable. They look like plain seams from the right side and small tucks from the wrong side.

Pin the wrong sides together and stitch a ¼-inch seam. Press the seam flat to one side. Trim the seam allowance to ⅛ inch. Turn the right sides together, fold, and press. Stitch on the seamline (¼ inch) to enclose raw edges.

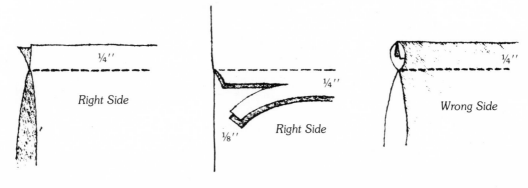

Right Side

¼″

Right Side

¼″

⅛″

Wrong Side

¼″

Cording

Cording is one of those special touches that customize many decorator projects. You can buy covered cording and the newer polyester braid cording in notions departments and fabric stores. You can also make your own quite easily by folding a bias strip over a length of cord, allowing ½-inch seam allowances on each side, and then stitching with a zipper foot. Don't squeeze the cord too tightly—another row of stitching will be added when the cording is enclosed in a seam.

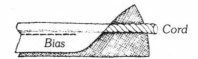

Cord

Bias

A Guide to Bias Yardage
1 yard of 36″ fabric = approx. 17 yards of seamed bias
1 yard of 45″ fabric = approx. 21 yards of seamed bias

Cutting Bias Strips

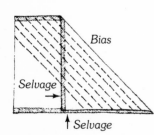

Bias

Selvage

Selvage

Fold the fabric on the true bias by folding one selvage perpendicular to the other. Press the fold. Measure, mark, and cut the bias strips as needed. If you will need a great amount of cording for a bedspread or another large project, it will be worth your time to make a bias sleeve so you can cut a continuous strip of bias.

1. Fold a length of fabric on true bias as shown in the illustration. Cut off the triangle formed.
2. Draw bias lines for as much cording as you will need. Cut off the excess fabric.

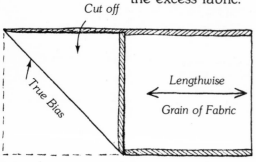

Cut off

True Bias

Lengthwise

Grain of Fabric

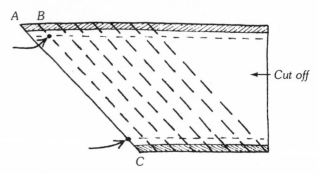

A   B

Cut off

C

3. Form a sleeve, right sides together, and pin the selvages together. Be sure to pin corner *C* to point *B*. Stitch with a ½-inch seam allowance. Press the seam and then cut along the lines starting at B/C and continuing in a spiral to the end of the sleeve.

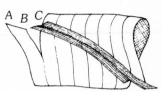

Joining the Bias
The bias is joined by placing two strips with the right sides together at right angles. Stitch a ½-inch seam allowance. Press open and trim off the corners if desired.

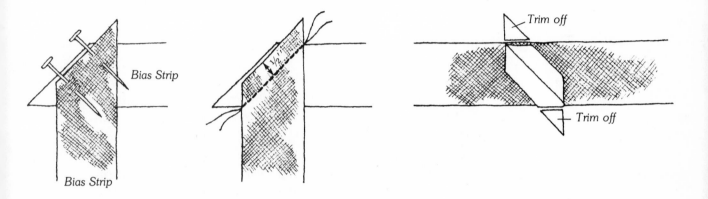

Joining the Cording
1. Cording is joined by cutting the covered cording ¾ inch longer than needed. Open the stitching on the bias, exposing the cords. Fold one end of the bias ½ inch to the inside and lap the raw edges of the other end over it. Trim the cords so that they just meet.
2. Reposition the bias into its original position. Stitch along the seam line.

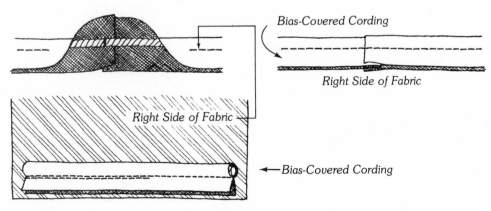

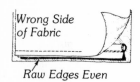

Wrong Side of Fabric

Raw Edges Even

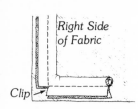

Right Side of Fabric

Clip

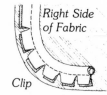

Right Side of Fabric

Clip

Enclosing Cording in Seams

1. Always start at a long edge, never at a corner.

2. Sew cording with the seam allowance of the cording lying on the seam allowance of the project. Then sew the facing or fabric piece on top to complete the seam and enclose the cording.

3. Corners can be squared or rounded. Lightweight fabrics will turn square corners quite easily. Heavy fabrics should be rounded. Medium-weight fabrics may work either way—the fabric will tell you. Curved edges are similar to rounded corners, but they require much more clipping to allow the cording to lie smooth and flat.

STAPLING

Stapling is one of the fastest, simplest, and least messy ways to apply fabric to a surface. The lightweight "tacker model" staple guns are often easiest to use since they can be activated with one hand, freeing the other hand to hold or stretch the fabric in place. Before buying a gun try it in your hand. Some models have a wide grip and are difficult for small hands to squeeze. Be sure you can hold the gun and shoot it quickly and easily. Recently, electric staple guns have been introduced by several manufacturers. They are activated at the touch of a button and shoot several staple lengths. They start at about $35.00 and are available in hardware stores and departments.

General Stapling Techniques

The basic techniques can be used on walls, tables, boxes, screens, wall hangings, and any other projects where stapling is practical.

1. Center the fabric and smooth it into place over the project. Use push pins to hold the fabric in place.

2. Start stapling in the center of one side and work to the ends.

3. Staple the opposite side in the same manner. Then staple the two remaining ends.

To keep tension even and the fabric smooth, it is important to work on opposite sides first. On many fabrics, staples are very inconspicuous and may even be left exposed on the right side if you wish. Or you may wish to try a quick camouflage trick: Paint or color staples to match the fabric background before loading them into the gun. Paint, shoe polish, or even a felt-tip pen will work.

Backtacking

If exposed staples are not acceptable to you, try backtacking. Follow these steps to make a backtacked seam:

1. Staple the fabric edge.

2. Lay the next fabric down on top of the first, aligning the design. Tack them with a few staples.

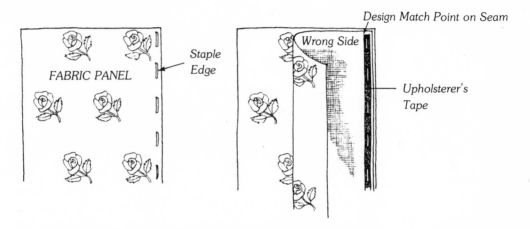

3. Lay a narrow piece of cardboard called upholsterer's tape (available at upholstery suppliers in strips or rolls) along the seam line and tack it in place.

4. Pull the fabric back against the upholsterer's tape and continue wrapping and stapling. The upholsterer's tape gives a firm, sharp edge and hides all of the staples.

To finish an edge, follow these steps.

1. Fold the fabric taut around a piece of upholsterer's tape and fasten the edge by pounding ½-inch wire brads in place. If the brads are concealed by fabric, pound them flat.

2. If the brads show, conceal them. Pound the brads in until $1/16$ inch is left exposed. Pick at the threads with a couple of pins until the fabric "swallows" the brad.

3. Pound the brad flat.

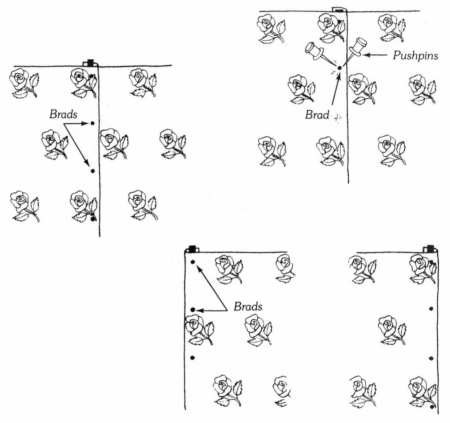

Staples can be removed easily from the fabric, which may then be reused if desired.

Hint: A layer of polyester fleece applied under the fabric gives a slightly upholstered look and at the same time opaques the fabric so the color or design on the original object won't show through. The fleece also protects the fabric covering from sharp blows and gives it a surface to "cling" to, creating a smoother appearance.

Fusible webs were used in the ready-to-wear industry for many years before being introduced to the home sewing market. Now widely available, the use of fusible webs has revolutionized sewing and decorating techniques. Once you use fusibles and begin to see their time-saving benefits, you'll wonder how you've survived without them.

Basically, fusibles are monofilaments in a random weblike pattern. They are very heat sensitive, 100 percent polyamide fibers. Fusible webs are sold by the yard in 18-inch widths, prepackaged in shorter lengths, or in convenient rolls of precut strips. The strips are handy for fusing hems, trims, and tacking down facings. It is most economical to cut your own strips from the wider yardage. Simply fold the webbing over and over into a roll. Then cut evenly through all layers. Unfold the roll and the strips are ready to use.

How the Fusibles Work

The webbing is placed between two objects, heat is applied, the webbing melts, and the two objects are then fused or "bonded" together. In decorating you may use fusibles to bond fabric to fabric or fabric to a nonfabric object. In a sense the fusible is a dry glue that you activate with heat to cause a bond between two objects. It should not be confused with iron-on fabrics, which have a bonding agent on one side enabling them to be ironed to a surface. The webbing itself melts completely when heat is applied, so it must be between the objects that are to be fused.

Inevitably, you'll get some fusible web on your iron from time to time. The easiest way to clean it off is to use one of the hot iron cleaners available in tubes in fabric notions departments. Cleaning is easiest while the iron is hot.

Fabric-to-Fabric Applications of Fusible Web

Always read the instructions that come with the webbing. They will tell you to use heat, moisture, pressure, and time. They should also add patience!

Heat . . . from an iron to melt the web.

Moisture . . . from an iron *plus* a damp press cloth. Moisture intensifies the heat. The cloth protects the iron from the fusible web and light-colored fabrics from a dirty iron.

Pressure . . . *not* a sliding, ironing motion. Use an up-down lift and set motion, which permits adequate heat to penetrate and melt the webbing. This type of motion also guards against stretching or distorting the fabric.

Time . . . Your iron must be placed in each position for the suggested length of time to create adequate heat on the web and make it melt. The length of time needed will vary with the weight of the fabric; 10 to 15 seconds is average. Every inch of the fabric must be covered, or there will be weak or unbonded spots. Overlapping with your iron ensures a good bond.

Patience . . . Your reward—a beautiful bond that is washable or dry cleanable, and no stitches showing. Improper bonds may loosen in washing or cleaning. It is worth the effort to do it right the first time. Resist the urge to peel the fabric and peek to see if a bond is taking. The bond sets as it cools.

Be sure to save scraps and pieces of the fusible webbing. They can be used on small places or when you have collected quite a supply, they can be overlapped "mosaic" style and fused as though they were one solid piece.

Examples of Bonding Fabric to Fabric
Hems
For fusing a 2-inch hem, turn up the hem and press. Insert the webbing strip in the hem 1¾ inch wide for a full-bodied hem, or ½ inch wide for a simple hem. Press only on the area where the webbing is placed. Avoid pressing the top edge of the hem, which can create a ridge on the front side. Be sure to press from both sides, following directions outlined previously.

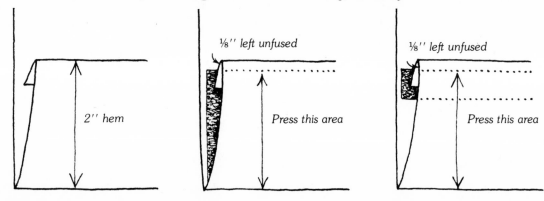

2'' hem   ⅛'' left unfused   Press this area   ⅛'' left unfused   Press this area

Appliqués

If you make your own appliqué from fabric, pin the webbing securely to the back of the fabric, with pins on the fabric side. Cut the two together and leave them pinned to prevent fabric or web from shifting. If you use a purchased appliqué, pin webbing to it, and carefully and accurately cut the webbing to fit. Position the appliqué on fabric. Touch the hot iron to a few places, in order to "baste" the appliqué in place. Carefully remove the pins. Lay a damp press cloth over appliqué. Steam and press for 10 to 15 seconds. Allow it to cool. Flip over the fabric and press on the wrong side, too. Raw edges on appliqués or other items may be zigzagged. However, if you cut the webbing carefully, keeping it the same size and not allowing it to shift, you may not need any edge finish.

Among the advantages of fusing appliqués or trims before zigzagging are the added body the fusible web gives and the fact that the appliqués will lie flat and smooth and will not ripple, pull, or twist while the finish stitching is done.

Hint: Wrap aluminum foil shiny side out around a piece of cardboard and place it on the ironing board as a base under the area being fused. It will help generate more heat when working with thick, hard-to-bond fabrics.

Fabric-to-Fabric Suggestions

This method is good for
- Hemming curtains, valances, shower curtains, table runners, and dust ruffles. It is also good for attaching appliqués, ribbons, braid, trims, and bias tape.
- A strip of webbing inside the side hem of curtains or draperies keeps the edges from "billowing" open at the window frame.
- After fusing the seam allowances down and then turning down the casing and stitching it in place, you can then insert curtain rods or elastic without getting caught under the seam allowances.
- It is possible to stiffen and strengthen fabric for cornices.
- You can use it to make roller shades.

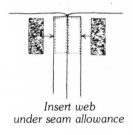

Insert web under seam allowance

Insert elastic or rod

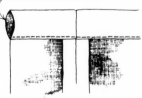

Fabric-to-Nonfabric Applications

Here comes the real excitement of decorating with fusibles. You can bond fabric to cardboard, wood, paper, metal, or almost any other non-heat-sensitive item. Since you will not be washing or cleaning these objects, you'll need less time and patience to get a good bond. You'll be amazed at how easy it is to cover objects this way. It is a durable and quite permanent way to cover an object with fabric.

To acquaint yourself with the ease of this technique, make a test sample or a small project or two. Before long you'll be covering and creating. Good projects include the following.

- Picture frames
- Folding screens
- Bookends or bookshelves
- Shelves
- Tables, cubes
- Desk accessories
- Line trunks (plain or patchwork style)
- Line or cover drawer fronts
- Lampshades
- Collage wall hangings
- Book covers

Note: If you need to splice on more fabric on projects, overlap the cut edges with fusible webbing in between, and then press them.

An Economical Alternative

As an alternative to commercial fusible webbing for some projects, plastic cleaner bags and even plastic wraps for food can be used as the fusible. Place the layer of plastic between the item to be covered and the fabric. Use as hot an iron as you dare. The plastic serves as the fusible. It won't melt completely, but it will melt enough to hold the fabric to wood or cardboard in particular.

This method should not be used on fabric-to-fabric application since it tends to deteriorate with time. However, the plastic may be used as a temporary fusible to hold fabric that is to be stitched down. For example, an appliqué may be "plastic fused" to position it. The zigzag or hand stitching secures it permanently. The plastic remains under the appliqué.

SPRAY GLUE

Aerosol spray glues can make quick work of many fabric projects. It is usually easiest to spray the glue on the fabric and apply the fabric to the object. This prevents getting glue where you don't want it, that is, on the inside of a lampshade or where it could attract dust and dirt.

Spread lots of paper, then place the fabric in the center. Spray the glue lightly and evenly. Use a slow motion to keep the glue under control. Too much wrist action can cause the glue to fly through the air and land on other objects in the room. Overspraying may cause the glue to soak through the fabric, so go lightly or make a test sample to determine penetration and holding power.

The fabric later can be stripped from the object, but a glue residue will remain, causing stiffness to the fabric and a tacky or rough surface on the object.

CRAFT OR WHITE GLUE

This type of glue is best when it is of the decorator craft variety, which is tackier and faster drying than ordinary general purpose white glues. That means it is less likely to soak through fabric. It is also more flexible when it dries, which is an advantage in fabric decorating.

Glue may be rolled, brushed, or spread on an object to be covered with fabric or trim. On walls or furniture involving large surfaces you may wish to dilute the glue with some water to make it go farther. In order to prevent the glue from soaking through, apply it, then allow it to become tacky to the touch. Finally, smooth the fabric in place. Edges may be cut or folded under, then allowed to dry.

Most fabrics can be stripped off at some later date. This will depend on the type of fabric and glue used.

LIQUID STARCH

Liquid starch, undiluted, may be used as a glue to apply fabric to many surfaces—for example, wood, metal, plastic, glass, plaster, wallboard, and concrete. Strange as it sounds, it really works. Always use liquid starch, not spray starch. I usually buy the premixed liquid. It is pink or blue, but the color does not affect the fabric. Occasionally I have mixed powdered starch with water to a consistency of medium white sauce and used this instead of the premixed starch.

Sponge the starch onto the object to be decorated, then smooth the fabric in place and trim to fit. For more holding power and a built-in soil-resistant finish, sponge the starch on top of the fabric, thoroughly soaking it. This helps reduce the tendency for bubbles to form. (If they do, just soak them flat with more starch.) When dry, the fabric is firm and crisp to the touch.

For small items like decals, ribbons, or trims, dip the fabric in the starch and smooth it into place, sponging off any excess starch. As a rule, a cut and overlapped edge is best. Folded edges tend to create bulk and may loosen. Handle cut and raw edges gently to prevent excess raveling. Don't pull ravels. Cut them off with sharp scissors or a razor blade.

To remove starched-on fabric just strip it off. Wash the surface of the object if a residue remains. The fabric will be stiff, but the starch may be washed out and the fabric reused. If the fabric is clinging so snugly that you fear it will pull off the paint when stripped, dampen it slightly with water on a sponge or in a spray bottle. The fabric will come off with no trouble at all.

Heavier and thicker fabrics require more starch during application because they absorb more. Starching is economical, however; half a gallon of starch often covers an eight-foot wall or more. Drips and spills are easier to clean up while damp, but even if they dry before you notice them, they can still be washed right off.

Check the label of your starch to see if it contains a mildew inhibitor. This is especially important if you plan to put the fabric in a bathroom or other potentially damp area. If a mildew inhibitor is not indicated, the addition of a small amount of disinfectant is helpful, or you can purchase from wallpaper stores a product that inhibits mildew.

Some brands of liquid starch contain salt, which can cause pitting and rusting of scissors, razor blades, and other metal objects if the starch is not rinsed off occasionally as you work. Take special care near hinges, door stops, metal trim near formica, and so on.

CELLULOSE OR VINYL WALLPAPER PASTE

Using this kind of paste is a fast and easy way to apply fabric to almost any surface. Wheat paste should be avoided, however, as it can cause staining on some fabrics. Vinyl paste is preferable for heavy-weight fabrics.

Sponge or roll wallpaper paste on the surface to be covered. Then smooth the fabric into place. The smoothing is important to reduce the tendency of bubbling as the fabric dries. A brush or wallpaper smoothing tool can be a help here.

Wallpaper pasted fabrics can be stripped off easily. Some paste residue will remain in the fabric and on the wall, but this can usually be washed out. If you are unsure of the type of paste you are using, make a test sample in a closet (for walls) or on a small object before beginning the larger project.

TWO

WALLS, CEILINGS, AND FLOORS

People have used fabrics or hangings to cover walls for a long time. First, fur robes warded off winter's chill and covered doors and windows. Then heavy tapestries provided insulation and beautification in drafty villas and castles. Fabric is still used on walls in much of Europe because of its durability and the fact that cracked or peeling plaster is easily concealed under fabric. Fabric is not as likely as wallpaper to split when walls settle a bit over the years. Even if you fabric a wall simply because you love the look, you will enjoy unexpected side benefits as well. It is hard to summarize all the advantages, some of which you will discover as you live with the completed project.

Walls do not have to be perfectly smooth, and they rarely need to be sized or specially prepared. Small cracks or minor unevenness can be covered and concealed easily by the fabric. Even the grooves in wall paneling are concealed by most fabrics. And since walls are seldom perfectly straight, you will appreciate the fact that fabrics can be eased or stretched slightly to fit perfectly. Because of their porosity and texture, fabrics can serve as insulators and acoustical aids as well.

You can use fabric in any room, but bedrooms, dining areas, and living rooms are the obvious choices because they get less wear and tear than bathrooms, halls, or kitchens. However, I have had fabric on walls in bathrooms for over four years with more years to come. I occasionally sponge off a few toothpaste splatters, but that is about all the care necessary. I have even had a cotton chintz starched to the toilet tank for three years with no problems at all. One of the nice things about fabric walls in a steamy bath is that the walls never run with moisture which condenses and then slides down smooth painted or tiled surfaces. Instead the fabric absorbs the moisture evenly, and the moisture then evaporates, leaving an unmarked wall covering.

You might expect to have to change fabric more often in a kitchen than in other places, but I have had students report that the same fabric lasted in their kitchens for nearly six years. Naturally it is wise to avoid the wall directly behind the range, or any other area that would be subject to greasy spatters.

Any wall surface—plaster, tile, concrete, plasterboard, or paneling—can be covered with fabric. Of course the construction of the wall will influence the method of application you choose. (Specific suggestions are given with each method later in this chapter.) But with a little thought you will see that anything is possible. For example, my bedroom has hard plaster walls that had been wallpapered and then painted with blue latex paint. I starched a blue and green bandana print right over the top with excellent results. In contrast, we wanted to put a wallpaper mural on a wall in another room, but didn't care for the idea of scraping or steaming the paper off at some later date. So I starched a couple of old worn sheets to the wall first. After allowing the fabric to dry I trimmed it along the floor, ceiling, and sides, and then papered the mural right over the sheets. Now we merely have to peel the sheets loose and everything will come off at once. This technique would also be useful in an apartment where you would like to remove the mural, leaving no traces of it, when you move.

You need not feel restricted to small all-over designs in fabric for larger surfaces. Let your imagination go. Even small rooms seem larger when lavishly decorated with a special fabric. Of course a large pattern will require more yardage to assure accurate matching.

Enjoy the mood created by a print or a design. You will find that you won't need so many objects or accessories to make a room feel finished. And a collection of items that looks cluttered against a plain background will hide itself against a pattern. Another way to achieve a feeling of space while using lots of pattern is to blend windows and furnishings into the total design by using the same fabric on them. Fabric also makes a perfect background for wall groupings or collections. The hanger holes won't show even when you relocate an object.

The fingerprints, scrapes, and marks that are all too obvious on painted walls just disappear. Perhaps it would be more appropriate to say that they just don't appear on most fabrics, because they are concealed in a busy print.

Certainly one of the questions most frequently asked about fabric decorating is, "Which will be more economical—fabric or wallpaper?" The answer depends on what the particular situation is, as well as your taste in fabric and your selection of paper. But remember, wall paper is usually 18 to 28 inches wide. Fabric is 36, 45, 48, 58, 60 inches wide, and, in the case of sheets, 66 to 108 inches wide. Wallpaper is purchased by the roll, often a double or triple roll. Fabric can be purchased in amounts closer to the quantity needed—as little as a fraction of a yard. Using fabric you have the advantage of using the same design for walls, curtains, roller shades, and pillows, so the dye lot will always match.

Perhaps the greatest advantage is that in most cases you can retrieve the fabric for another use when you choose to remove it and redecorate, or when you move. This factor really should be considered when you think of the overall investment.

Before You Begin

Get acquainted with the room and with the fabric. Consider where you will put the fabric. You may want to cover all four walls, highlight one wall, accent a dormer or alcove, or experiment with the ceiling or floor. Remember that bathrooms are usually small but somewhat complicated because of the number of objects around which the fabric must be fitted. You'll learn a lot in a short time.

Measure the area to be covered. This gives you a rough idea of the amount of yardage needed and also indicates if the walls and

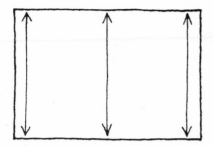 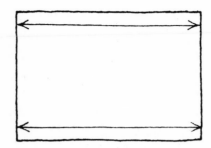

the ceiling are straight. Measure at the points indicated by arrows in the illustration.

Fabrics with horizontal stripes or obviously horizontal design motifs can call attention to an uneven ceiling. All-over prints and drop match designs are less affected by this problem, as shown here.

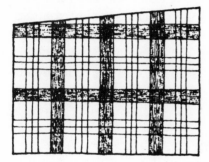 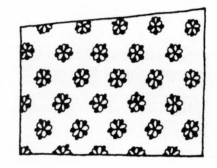

MAKE A TEST SAMPLE

Making a test sample may seem unimportant or even a waste of time, but it is not. Sometimes we are buoyed by the success of a completed project, and plunge into the next, assuming another fabric will work exactly the same way as the first. It may, but it may not. The time and money spent on a test sample are worth it when you consider the yards of fabric and the amount of patience at stake. The test sample will tell you a lot about the fabric and about the method or methods of application, you are considering. Make the test in an inconspicuous spot—in a closet, a hall, basement, an area low on the wall, or behind a door—wherever the surface is the same as the one you plan to cover. Two or three pieces of fabric, each at least a foot square (the larger the better), will enable you to test a fabric's ability to:

- Conceal texture on walls and grooves on paneling
- Cover paint color or the wallpaper pattern beneath
- Hold to the wall surface
- Resist shrinking or color fading
- Conceal staples

Be sure to include at least a couple of seam finish techniques in the test sample so you will be able to check for shrinkage as well as ease of cutting, butting, overlapping, or backtacking a seam.

MEASURING

Determining the amount of fabric you need is not difficult if you measure step by step. A pocket calculator will simplify matters considerably. Begin by thinking in terms of the number of fabric strips or panels you will need to cover the area you have chosen. The diagram shows that nine fabric strips would be required to cover this room.

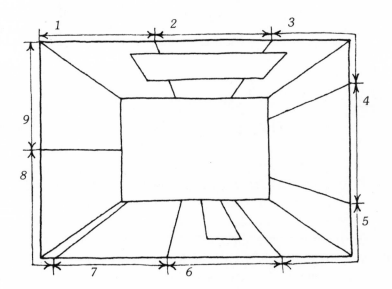

Step One—Determining the Number of Panels

1. Add the corner-to-corner measurements of the walls to be covered.

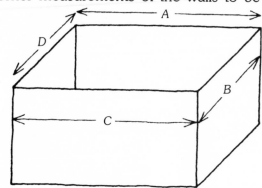

(A)_____ inches
(B)_____ inches
(C)_____ inches
(D)_____ inches

_____

(E)_____ Total inches

Note: For ceiling or floors measure across direction panels will be applied.

2. (E) ÷ usable width of fabric in inches = (F) number of panels needed*

*Add an extra panel if the number is uneven. For example, $6 + 24'' = 7$ panels.

Measure the actual usable inches of design. This eliminates selvages and overlap.

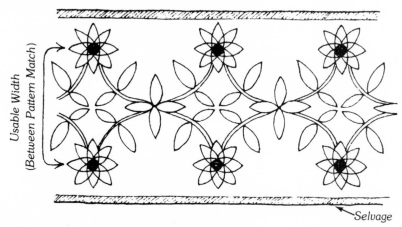

Usable Width
(Between Pattern Match)

Selvage

Step Two—Determining Panel Length

1. Measure ceiling to baseboard.

(G) _____ inches

For a ceiling or floor measure with the direction panels will be applied.

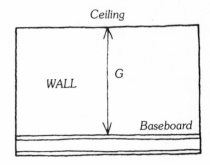

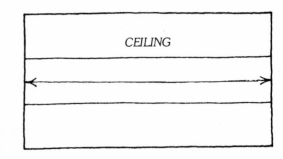

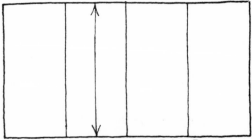

Direction of Fabric Panel

2. Measure the distance between the design repeat and add that to the wall height.

(H) _____ inches

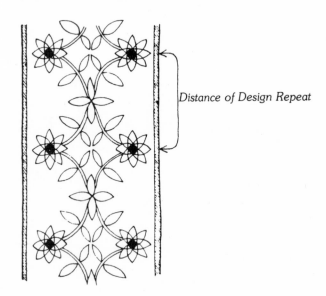

Distance of Design Repeat

3. (I) <u>3</u> inches   Add 3 inches to the length of each panel for handling ease. *Note:* I usually do not subtract for doors and windows unless there are many, they are large, and occupy space nearly floor to ceiling. This means some extra fabric pieces are left over, but they are great for pillows or other small projects.

4. Total the measurements in items 1 through 3.

   (G)_____ inches

   (H)_____ inches

   (I)_____ inches

   (J)_____ Panel length in inches

Step Three—Converting Panel Lengths to Yards

1. $(J) \times (F) = (K)$ Total Inches Needed. Multiply panel length (J) times the number of panels (F) to determine the total inches of fabric needed.

2.   <u>(L) No. of Yards</u>

  36'')(K) total inches

Divide the total length (K) by 36 inches to determine the yards of fabric needed. It is a good idea to add a yard or two for leeway, and more if you are planning to make curtains, shades, and so on.

Where To Start

If your fabric has a design that clearly requires centering in the area to be covered, begin in the center of the most conspicuous wall and work in both directions. For example, a good starting spot may be behind the sofa, or over a fireplace. If the pattern does not require centering it is easiest to pick the least conspicuous corner or area and begin there. Thus if you wrap the fabric around the room and return to this starting point, you will be at the least noticeable point to finish off the last seam, which usually will not match. Be sure to start the first strip so that the pattern design is symmetrical at the ceiling line. Determine this placement before you start cutting panel lengths.

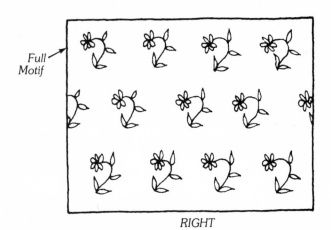

*Full
Motif*

RIGHT

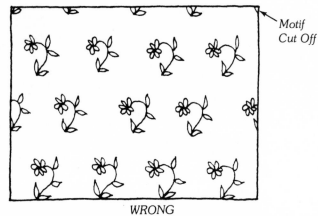

*Motif
Cut Off*

WRONG

PLUMB LINES

No matter what method of fabric or application you choose, establishing a plumb line as you proceed along the wall will help keep the fabric panels straight. Attach a string to a plumb bob or heavy object such as a pair of scissors. Rub the cord with chalk and attach it to the top of the wall along the edge of the first panel. Hold the weight at the baseboard and snap the line against the wall. The vertical chalk mark is your guide.

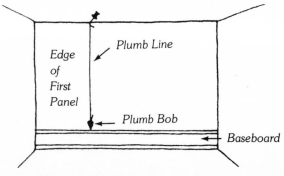

*Edge
of
First
Panel*

Plumb Line

Plumb Bob

Baseboard

Note: You do not *have* to chalk the string, but it is very helpful. You may just hang the plumb line along the panel and leave it as you work. I plumb each panel I apply. This assures getting each panel straight without stretching it.

PUSH PINS

Push pins hold the fabric in place while you get it straight and as you apply it to the wall. When you work with starch or paste methods, it helps to move the pins down the wall as you work, keeping the fabric from coming down on your head if you tug too hard. A strip of double-faced tape may work if the walls are too hard for push pins. If you have picture molding around the ceiling, you may cut small slits in the handling allowance of the fabric and hang it from molding hooks while you work, or pin the fabric to the molding.

Eight Ways to Fabric Walls

STAPLING

Stapling is an easy way to apply fabric to walls, especially if the walls are made of plasterboard or wood. Fabric may be stapled directly to the wall (staples exposed or covered), backtacked to conceal staples, or applied to furring strips. Furring strips help conceal rough or uneven walls and also make it possible to staple to plaster or concrete. You will be surprised at how much texture can be covered effectively by stapling fabric to walls.

A coat of paint will fill old staple holes—so fabric now, paint later.

Stapling Directly to the Wall

1. Cut fabric panels the desired length. Add 3 inches for handling ease. Be sure to match the pattern before you cut each panel. Review general stapling techniques from previous chapter and determine whether you will want to conceal staples by coloring or backtacking.

2. Determine the position of the first panel and establish a plumb line.

3. Start at the top. Use push pins or double-faced tape to hold fabric.

4. Staple at the top every 2 or 3 inches close to the ceiling.

5. When the fabric is secure, pull at the bottom opposite each staple at the top, keeping fabric taut and smooth but not over-stretched. Staple the bottom piece in place.

6. Staple first one side and then the other.

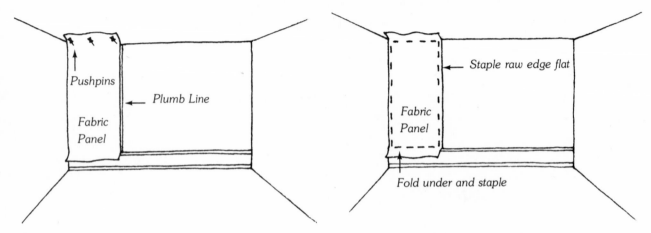

7. Using push pins overlap the next panel flat or with the edge folded under and staple the seam. Staple the top, bottom, and the side. Continue with succeeding panels.

8. Cut off any excess fabric at the ceiling and floor with a sharp razor blade, using a metal straight edge as a guide. If you prefer, you may turn the edges under at the top and bottom and staple them in place.

9. Ceiling (and floor) edges may be covered with braid trim, fabric border, piping, or moldings if desired. Or all edges and seams may be accented and covered with wood strips or "beams." To make beams, sand and paint boards. Position the ceiling strip first and then the floor strip; do the vertical strips last. Boards may be flat against the wall or they can stand away, depending on the effect you desire. You do not have to match the pattern design as carefully with this method. Since the beams will hide the edges, selvages can often be butted together.

Furring Strips

Furring strips are thin wood strips (usually 1 x ¼ inch) that are used as a buffer. Fabric can be stretched and stapled to the strips, thus allowing rough or uneven walls to be covered. They can also be attached to concrete or hard plaster walls with nails or paneling adhesive. You can purchase furring strips at a local lumberyard, or make them yourself from heavier lumber.

1. Apply furring strips to the wall horizontally, along ceiling, floor, each side of a corner, and vertically where the seams will be. Outline the doors and windows as shown in the illustration.

2. Attach the fabric to the furring strips by one of the methods described previously under stapling. If desired, trim edges with gimp or double welting for an elegant touch.

Note: Professional decorators often "upholster" a wall by stapling heavy flannel or ½-inch thick fireproof dacron to the furring strips first, seaming and stapling fabric panels to the wall.

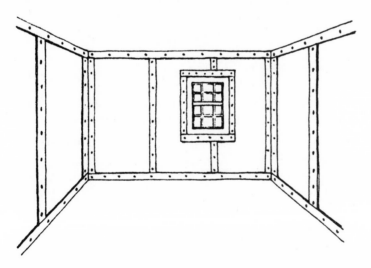

Seamed Panels

It is possible to seam the fabric lengths together before applying them to a wall. The main difficulties are getting good, even tension on the fabric and handling the large panel thus created. To combat the former you may want to staple the fabric in place along the ceiling and let it hang for 24 hours, allowing the fabric to stretch to accommodate its weight. To solve the latter problem,

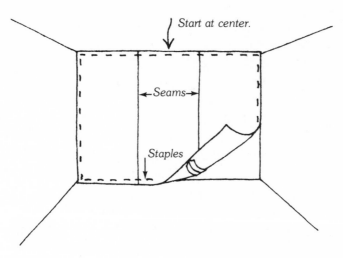

ask someone to help you apply the fabric. This may create other problems. One of my students told me that she and her husband had applied fabric this way. "Did you find it easy?" I inquired. "No, it almost ended in divorce," she laughed, "but it looked terrific when it was finished."

STARCHING

This is my own favorite method for applying fabric. It is a little messy, but it does a super job and has many advantages.

• Starching leaves fewer bubbles in the fabric than using wallpaper paste.

• Starched fabric can be peeled off the wall when you want a change, and the fabric can be washed and used again.

• Starch provides a built-in, soil-resistant finish so that a simple sponging with soap and water, spot lifter, or cleaning fluid removes most spots.

• Walls don't have to be sized or prepared as long as they can withstand moisture (untreated plaster or drywall should be sealed) and are not heavily soiled or greasy.

What Fabric Works Best?

Only a test sample will give you the final answer, but I have found that cotton chintz works superbly because it is firm and slightly glazed (which helps it to shed stains and soil). Because cotton is absorbent it holds the most firmly of all fabrics. Other cotton blends work well too, but the more cotton content, the better.

Starching a Wall

1. Sponge off the wall if it is very soiled or to remove greasy film.

2. Cut the fabric panels to the desired length, including pattern match and handling ease. Trim off the firmly woven portion of the selvage if it has been pulled or distorted in the printing process.

3. If the pattern match is more than 1 inch from the edge, trim off the excess, leaving no more than 1 inch of overlap.

4. Determine the placement of the first panel. Establish a plumb line. (Because of the stretchy nature of some fabrics it is wise to plumb each panel.) Protect the floor with plastic.

5. Pour starch into a pan. Dip the sponge and saturate it with starch. Then apply liberally to the wall for the first several feet.

6. Smooth the fabric into place at the top of the wall, leaving about 1 inch to be trimmed later. Use push pins to hold the fabric temporarily as you work your way down the panel, adding starch underneath by lifting the panel when needed. Smooth the panel with the grain in a vertical motion.

7. Now apply starch to the top surface of the panel, smoothing the fabric in place with a vertical motion to remove bubbles and wrinkles and to prevent stretching. Be sure the starch penetrates the fabric evenly. This step also ensures a smooth soil-resistant finish.

8. Work your way down the panel, continuing to sponge starch onto the wall, smoothing the fabric, and applying more starch.

9. Position the second panel, matching the design along the edge. Treat the seam by overlapping, lapping and cutting, or butting. (These finishes are illustrated later in this chapter.)

10. Seams are cut while fabric is damp. However, excess fabric should be cut at the floor and ceiling and around doors and windows when it has dried completely. It will then cut clean like paper. Any shrinkage will have occurred before you trim. If you make an accidental cut while trimming starch the pieces back

together, let it dry and then trim it again. The patched spot will be nearly invisible.

11. Continue with succeeding panels. If you are wrapping two or more walls, smooth the fabric into the corner and onto the next wall, plumbing the edge before you start the next panel. Smooth and tug fabric into line if needed. It is easier to wipe up excess starch from ceiling, baseboards, or window frames as you go, before it dries.

If some bubbles are evident when the fabric has dried, soak them with starch and smooth them out. This is most likely to happen with medium and heavier fabrics.

Removing Fabric

To remove starched-on fabric from a wall, peel one corner loose and then gently peel the fabric panel off. If the fabric is holding very snugly and you are concerned that it may pull off some paint, just moisten the fabric with a damp sponge or spray bottle and continue to peel it loose. When the fabric is damp it will strip smoothly and evenly. The same removal technique applies when using wallpaper paste.

CELLULOSE WALLPAPER PASTE

Shiny, slick walls may need to be roughened with sandpaper or sized first with paint or a product from the wallpaper store, which increases the holding power of the paste, but most will require no preparation.

1. Prepare the wall if necessary and cut the panels of fabric. Match the design before cutting. Establish a plumb line on the wall. Usually it is wise to plumb each panel.

2. Mix the paste following package directions. Brush or roll it directly onto the wall, approximately the width of the panel and 3 to 4 feet deep.

3. Press the fabric into place and smooth it with your hands and a smooth object such as a wallpaper brush or roller. Leave 1 inch excess at the ceiling, at the baseboard, and around doors,

windows, switches, and so on, to be trimmed away later when the fabric is dry.

4. Handle the seams according to method you have chosen.

5. Wipe excess paste off seams, baseboards, and other messy edges.

6. Complete final trimming when the fabric is completely dry.

VINYL WALLPAPER PASTE

Premixed vinyl wallpaper paste has excellent holding power for fabrics, especially heavier types. It is a relatively expensive method for applying fabric, but very easy. As always, make a test sample to determine holding power and stripability. Follow the directions for using cellulose paste. Be careful to keep the paste off the surface of the fabric.

GLUING

White glues can also be used to apply fabric to walls. They are fairly permanent and have excellent holding power on most surfaces, but you may remove some paint when the fabric is stripped off. The white glue method gives fabric some tendency to bubble if it is not smoothed well.

1. Prepare the fabric panels and plumb the wall.

2. Dilute the glue one to one with water. Apply the glue mixture with a paintbrush or roller using the same procedure as for wallpaper paste.

3. Smooth the fabric into place; brush and smooth out all wrinkles and bubbles.

4. Handle the seams according to the method you have chosen.

5. Wash up spills or drips as you go along. Trim excess fabric when it is almost dry. Be sure to sponge off any excess glue mixture before it dries.

SHIRRING

You can achieve an elegant wall treatment using shirred or gathered fabric. This technique is also practical because it will conceal a texture or pattern already on the walls. Architectural problems (doors or pipes for example) can also be easily covered. In addition, you have yards of fabric for later use when you re-decorate.

Although the technique requires a large amount of fabric, it is relatively easy to install shirred or gathered fabric panels. The panels need not be seamed together, since the edges can easily be hidden in the gathers.

Figuring the Yardage
1. Width of all _____ x fullness desired * _____
   = _____ Total Width

*2x is standard; many prefer 2½x; 3x is quite full but best for sheer fabric.

2. Total Width _____ ÷ Width of Fabric _____
   = Number of Panels

3. Floor to ceiling measurement _____ inches
   Allowance for top and bottom hems +6 inches
   Take up when rods are inserted in casing +1 inch

   Panel Length _____ inches

4. Panel length _____ X number of panels _____
   = _____ Yardage in inches

5. Yardage in inches _____ ÷36″
   = _____ Number of yards needed

Note: Matching the design at the selvage is not quite as important with this method because the design is disguised by the gathers, but additional yardage should be included since matching will give a more professional look.

Sheets are a natural for this method because of their light weight and their width.

Figuring the Number of Sheets:

1. Width of wall _____ inches x fullness desired _____ = _____ Inches total width.

2. Total width _____ inches ÷ Width of sheet you will use _____ inches = _____ Number of sheets.

Preparing the Fabric

1. Turn the hem edge under 3 inches and press. Turn the raw edge under ½ inch and machine stitch the hem in place.

2. Run another row of stitches across the panel 1½ inches from the fold. Repeat at the bottom.

Note: If you use sheets, try to use the stitched hems in one casing or heading.

Installation

1. Install café curtain brackets and rods at intervals along the ceiling and the floor, above and below windows, and above doors as necessary. Shirr fabric panels onto the rods. Hang the rods in brackets and adjust the gathers for evenness. (Extension brackets can be used to hold fabric away from the wall to clear pipes or other concealed objects.) *OR*

2. Thread half round molding (from a lumber dealer) through the hem casings, adjust gathers, and nail the molding directly into the walls at regular intervals. Stretch the fabric into place near the floor and nail it into place. This results in a neat but more permanent installation. *OR*

3. Fabric may be attached directly to the wall with staples after you have shirred it with shirring tape. Allow 4 inches for top and bottom hems. Stitch the hems and tape as indicated. Pull the cords to shirr the fabric. Staple it to the wall. *OR*

4. Measure and cut the fabric as you did for the previous methods, but fold under ¾ inch, thus making a ¾-inch casing. Attach a cord to a screw hook or nail in the wall. Run the cord through the casing. Attach the cord firmly to the opposite wall in

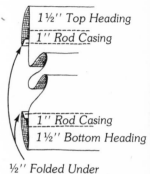

1½'' Top Heading
1'' Rod Casing
1'' Rod Casing
1½'' Bottom Heading

½'' Folded Under and Stitched Down

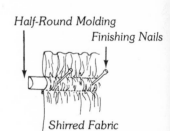

Half-Round Molding
Finishing Nails
Shirred Fabric

1½'' Heading
Wrong Side
2-Cord
Shirring Tape

1½'' Heading
¾'' Casing

the same manner. Fabric can be stapled directly to the wall at regular intervals after the gathers are distributed evenly.

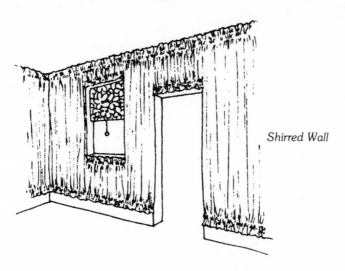

Shirred Wall

DOUBLE-FACED TAPE

Double-faced tape, such as masking tape or carpet tape, can be used to attach fabric to walls. (Be sure to read the directions. Some tapes remove paint and even wood when stripped off.)

1. Apply tape at the ceiling line, floor, and two strips in each corner (one on each side). Place a strip around door and window openings. Apply vertical strips where the edges of each fabric length will form a seam on the wall. (edges of fabric should butt, not overlap.) Do not remove the protective covering strip on the tape at this time.
2. Starting in one corner of the ceiling, remove the paper from the adhesive for one width of fabric. Smooth the fabric over the tape.
3. Remove the paper from the corner strip about 12 inches at a time. Smooth the fabric over the adhesive. Repeat on the other side, keeping the fabric taut.

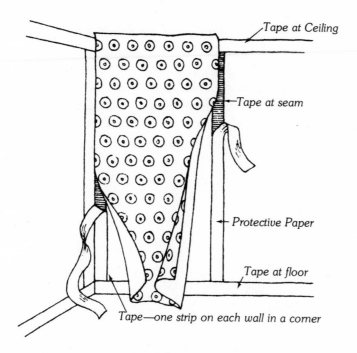

Tape at Ceiling

Tape at seam

Protective Paper

Tape at floor

Tape—one strip on each wall in a corner

4. Stretch and press the fabric onto bottom tape a little at a time, lining up the weave or pattern. Trim the surplus later.

5. Repeat with the second fabric length. Match the pattern on the seams and butt edges of the second fabric length to the first panel.

6. Repeat around doors and windows, trimming away surplus fabric. The tape will hold down the raw edges.

7. When all the surfaces are covered, trim excess fabric with a sharp blade.

WRAPPED PANELS

By wrapping panels with fabric and setting them in place along the wall, you can avoid putting fabric on the wall itself. This is also a good technique for concealing rough or damaged walls.

1. Cut fiberboard or damaged wall paneling to the ceiling height to fit a wall area.

2. Wrap the fabric around the panels and staple or tape it into place.

3. Set the panels into place along the wall and fasten them with a finishing nail at each corner. (Nail holes can be spackled and filled later if panels are removed.) If the panels are cut carefully to fit from the floor to the ceiling, sometimes they can be pushed and wedged into place without using nails.

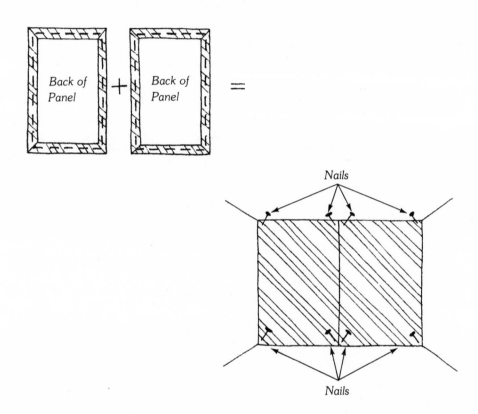

VINYL- OR MYLAR™-WRAPPED PANELS

If you want to wrap vinyl or vinyl-backed Mylar™ (available in silver, gold, or copper in 54 inch widths) snugly around a panel and apply it to a wall or use as a table top, select a flexible board such as Upson board® as a base. Do not try to use foamboard or cardboard as they will crease.

1. First staple the vinyl along the long edge of the panel.
2. Then lift the panel and slip a rug tube or plastic pipe under the panel, making it bow slightly.
3. Pull the second long edge snugly over the panel and staple.
4. Pull the tube out and push down on the panel, flattening it and pulling the vinyl taut.
5. Finally, staple the short ends.

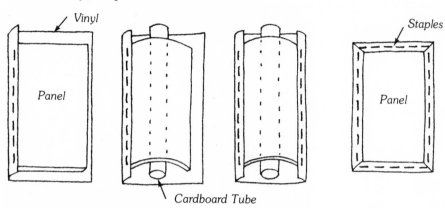

Vinyl · Panel · Staples · Panel · Cardboard Tube

MOLDING-TRIMMED FABRIC PANELS

Apply fabric to a section of wall and then outline the panels with wood molding or braid trim. Also try fabric panels on doors, cupboards, drawers, and so on. If molding is already in place on the object, you may remove it, apply the fabric and then replace the molding. Or you can cut fabric to fit inside the molding and use wallpaper paste or starch to apply it.

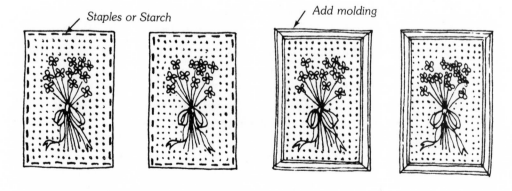

Staples or Starch · Add molding

SOFFITS

The space between kitchen cupboards and the ceiling is an easy and obvious place for fabric. Be sure to measure the soffit height in several places before you begin, as soffits are often very uneven.

Cut the bottom edge of the fabric smoothly with scissors, allowing 1 inch extra at the ceiling to be trimmed off later when the fabric is dry. If your soffit is even, cut the fabric piece to fit and put it in place.

Ceilings and floors can be fabric covered, too!

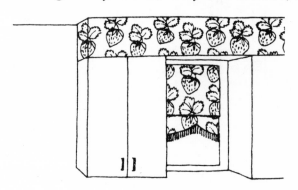

Fabric Ceilings

Not only are fabric-covered ceilings spectacular, they can help conceal chipped or cracked plaster, rough or uneven ceilings, or peeling paint. Fabric can also alter the apparent height of a ceiling.

Whatever method of application you choose, covering a ceiling with fabric requires assistance in order to make the job easier and safer. Review the directions for figuring yardage, being sure to determine which way the fabric will run. Additional length will be necessary for any suspended technique you choose.

DIRECT APPLICATION

Smooth Firm Ceilings
Fabric may be applied with starch, glue, wallpaper paste, or staples. Follow directions for applying fabrics to walls. It may be helpful to roll the fabric onto a tube, unrolling it carefully and smoothing it into place as you move along the ceiling.

Textured or Soft Ceilings
Apply furring strips around the perimeter of the ceiling and at each place where there will be a seam in the fabric. Then staple the fabric to the furring strips, stretching it flat and taut.

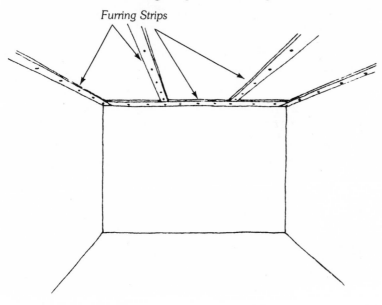

Furring Strips

Flat Shirred Fabric
Because of the weight of the fabric it may be necessary to use several strips of rods across a very wide ceiling in order to keep the fabric from sagging. Install the rods and shirr fabric in the same way as for walls.

SUSPENDED APPLICATION

Fabric may be draped flat across the ceiling, but it can be especially effective if shirred for added softness.

1. Attach dowels or café curtain rods to the wall. Use curtain brackets, cup hooks, screw hooks, or screw eyes to hold the rods. Run the rods along the center of the ceiling, too. Drape the fabric across the rod or run the rod through a casing stitched in the fabric, nailing through the rod to hold the fabric in place. Multiple draping can also be achieved by placing more rods across the ceiling at regular intervals. It is also possible to achieve this look by draping the fabric to furring strips and then stapling, rather than using the rods.

2. Fabric can be draped and stapled directly to beams on open-rafter ceilings.

Idea: Low wattage lighting above a patchwork ceiling gives a stained glass effect. Be sure to allow for air circulation and keep fabric away from bulbs to prevent a fire hazard. It is also a good idea to treat the fabric with a fire-retardant liquid, available in hardware stores.

Fabric-Covered Floors

For an exciting and different effect, fabric a floor. The resulting application will be quite permanent, but can be covered with carpeting or a new floor covering at a later date. A fabric-covered floor can withstand a great deal of abuse if it is prepared properly.

1. Measure the floor and determine fabric yardage.

2. Clean the floor completely. Use a grease remover such as trisodium phosphate, and be sure the floor is vacuumed well.

3. Measure and determine the center of the floor. Mark location for the first panel.

4. Center the first panel and apply it to the floor with starch or

white glue diluted with a little water. Use the butt technique on seams. Be sure to cut off all ravelings with a sharp razor blade before they dry.

5. Allow the fabric to dry completely, then:

• Apply two coats of shellac and three light coats of varnish. Allow fabric to dry thoroughly (at least overnight) between each coat. *OR*

• Apply several light coats of polyurethane finish. Allow to dry overnight between each coat. (This may chip more easily than the previous method.) *OR*

• Use an epoxy-type sealer (such as is used for gym floors). This will give a very glossy, smooth finish.

The Important Details

Here is a potpourri of tips and techniques to help take the guesswork and frustration out of your projects.

SEAMS

Techniques covered in this section relate to damp methods such as glue, paste, and starch. Basically, I have found three ways of handling seams—overlapping, overlap and cut, and butted. You will find which is best and easiest for a particular fabric by including a seam or two in your test sample.

Overlapping (The Landlord Seam)

With firm, lightweight fabric (for example, chintz, broadcloth), overlapping may be satisfactory. I personally prefer methods with no lump or ridge at the seams. However, in apartments or rentals this may be the best method since it makes no marks on the walls. It has one other advantage—since the seam is not cut back to the pattern match, the fabric may be removed from the wall, washed, and used for another project where seams could then be sewn, lapped and cut, or backtacked.

On most fabrics the design match is printed at or near the selvage. The seam can be easily overlapped and matched. On some fabrics the match may be 2 to 3 inches from the edge. Thus, to overlap a seam easily and achieve an accurate match, the excess should be trimmed off, leaving about ½ inch beyond the match.

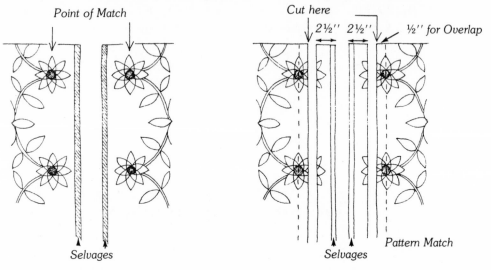

Overlap and Cut

This is a professional seam that is easy to do. It's best for fabrics you can see through while working and fabrics that tend to ravel easily.

1. If necessary, trim off excess fabric to create about 1 inch of overlap.

2. Apply fabric to the wall, being careful to match the design. On many lighter fabrics you will be able to see through the top layer while it is wet, thus making it easier to align it with the design beneath. Smooth the overlap into place.

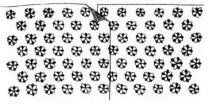

3. Allow seam to "set" for about a half hour or so before cutting. This allows time for some shrinkage and relaxation. The seam must be cut while it is still damp and flexible, but there will be ample time. Meanwhile you can proceed with succeeding pan-

els. To cut the seam use a sharp single-edged razor blade. To prevent "chewing" the fabric, discard blades as they dull.

4. Cut through the middle of the overlap with firm pressure. You must cut through both layers of fabric. (Using a ruler is optional here.)

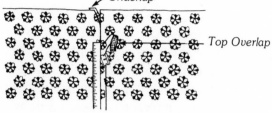

5. Peel off the top overlap strip of fabric and discard it.

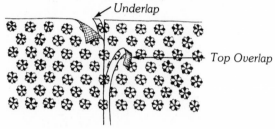

6. Slightly lift the top layer, reach inside and gently peel out the underlap.

7. Smooth the cut edges together, applying a little starch if necessary.

If some shrinkage occurs and the edges separate a bit, apply a little more starch and push them back. If you can get them to dry together, they stay together. (Your test sample will have shown you how much shrinkage to expect in your fabric.)

Butted Seams

Sometimes it is best or easiest to butt seams together. Fabrics that warrant this treatment include:

• Fabrics with a white selvage adjacent to the pattern match.

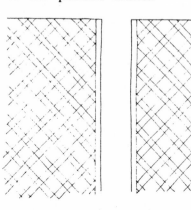

Lapping and cutting this fabric is difficult since it is unlikely you can overlap and cut without leaving some of the white selvage in the seam finish.

• Fabrics dark in color or heavy enough that you can't see through them when they are wet.

1. Apply the fabric panel to the wall, following the plumb line to keep the edges even and straight.

2. Using a metal edge ruler and a sharp razor blade, trim off the selvage and lap through the center of the design match. (Cutting the strip after applying to the wall means less chance of raveling the edge.)

3. With sharp scissors, carefully cut the excess lap from the next adjoining panel. Be sure to cut right at the pattern match.

Pattern Match

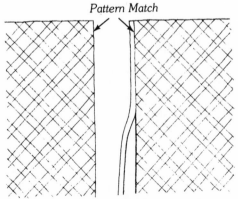

4. Butt the cut edges together. Match the design, working and smoothing the fabric into place. Then work your way across the rest of the panel.

Wallpaper Corners

When putting fabric on a wall that has been wallpapered, it is not desirable to cut with a razor at the corners, since the blade would cut through the paper, opening up the corner to view. Instead, use a yardstick and tailor's chalk to draw a line on the fabric in the corner. Peel the fabric back a little and cut carefully with sharp scissors. Smooth fabric back into place.

Ravelings

Ravelings may occur along the cut edges. Do not pull them. Cut them off with a sharp razor blade held firmly at the seam, then pull raveling, against the cutting edge. *Raveling*

GOING AROUND AND OVER

Doors and Windows with Frames

Leave the fabric uncut as long as possible if it is convenient to handle. Smooth it up to the door or window opening and secure with push pins as needed. Cut away excess fabric, leaving at least 1 inch of fabric overlapping the frame. Clip at the corner to fit fabric.

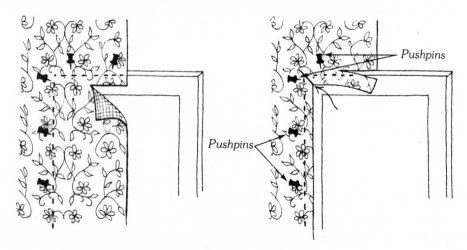

Pushpins

Pushpins

Finishing (Starch or Paste Methods)
Smooth fabric up close to the framework. Allow it to dry completely. Use a sharp razor blade and metal straight edge to cut the fabric cleanly near the frame. Peel away the fabric strip.

Finishing (Stapling Method)
Fold the 1-inch edge under so it fits snugly against the doorway or window. Staple the fabric directly to the wall, keeping the staples close to the frame. Or you can put strips of double-faced tape around the opening. Smooth the fabric onto the tape and trim it with a razor blade. Another way is to use upholsterer's tape and finish off with brads.

Arches and Recessed Windows and Doorways
First Method
The easiest way to handle these architectural features is to paint the inside of the area, bringing the paint around to lap ½ inch onto the wall so you can get a clean line when you trim the fabric ⅛ to ¼ inch from the edge to prevent fraying or peeling. Use a sharp blade and a metal straight edge as a guide.

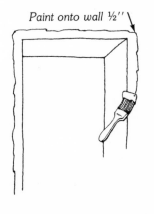

Paint onto wall ½″

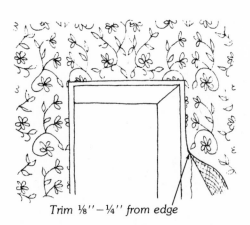

Trim ⅛″ – ¼″ from edge

If you have trouble cutting the fabric evenly with a razor blade, position the fabric so that it overlaps the edge of the doorway. Then mark the fabric by running a pencil or piece of tailor's chalk along the edge of the doorway. Lift the fabric a little. Then, using a sharp pair of scissors, cut evenly ⅛ to ¼ inch from the line marked at the edge of the doorway.

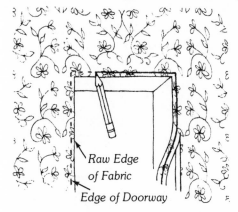

Raw Edge
of Fabric

Edge of Doorway

Second Method

Another way to handle this problem is to wrap the fabric around onto the inside of the recess by about ½ inch. Clip curves and smooth to fit when necessary. Cut a matching strip of fabric ¼ inch less than the width of the inside of the arch. Cut the strip long enough to start from the middle of the inside top, then down each side where the strip will match with the adjacent wall. The mismatch with the center top will not detract.

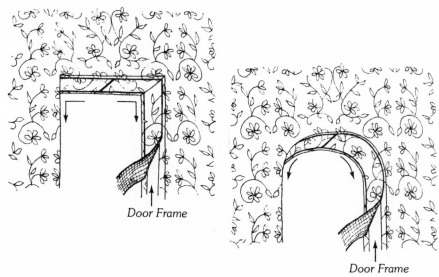

Door Frame

Door Frame

Third Method

Here is a slightly more complicated method, which allows for a pattern match on all sides of the recessed opening.

1. Hang the fabric in usual way, overlapping the door or window area. With scissors, make a horizontal cut in the strip, stopping 1 inch from the edge of the window recess.

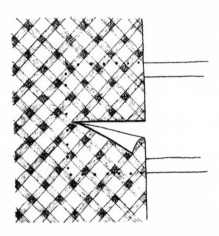

2. Cut up vertically and then to the corner at a 45° angle. Make another cut downward in the same way. Press the top and bottom strips smoothly onto the recess edges. Press the narrow vertical flap onto the edge of the recess.

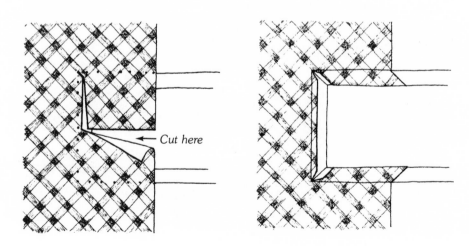

← *Cut here*

3. Measure and cut a matching strip of fabric to cover the sides of the opening. The piece should be as wide as the recess and long enough to cover the 1″ gap at the top and bottom of the recess.

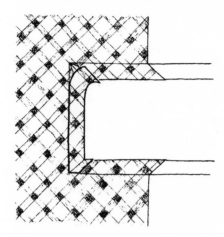

Objects that Project from the Wall or Ceiling

When an object projects several inches from the wall or ceiling, it is difficult to apply fabric over it accurately. You may need to make a clean cut from the nearest or least conspicuous edge, and then cut away excess fabric. When two or more objects are adjacent in the center of a fabric panel, cut through the shortest distance to one object and clip around it, then trim fabric to fit around the second object.

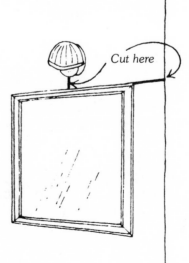

Cut here

To wrap fabric around a pipe or round fixture, make a clean cut through the fabric from either the shortest or the least conspicuous edge. Then make a series of cuts, and fit the fabric around the object. When the fabric is dry, trim around the object with a sharp razor blade.

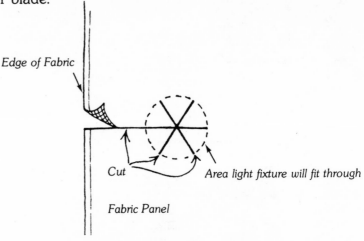

Edge of Fabric

Cut

Area light fixture will fit through

Fabric Panel

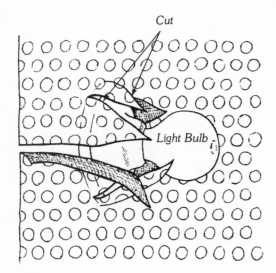

Cut

Light Bulb

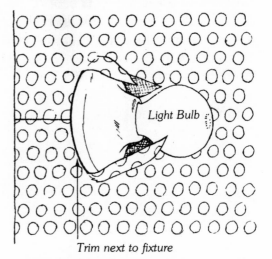

Light Bulb

Trim next to fixture

Small Objects

Small objects, such as clips for towel bar holders, toothbrush holders, or nails for pictures, may be covered over with fabric. Then slit the fabric with a razor blade, allowing the object to slip

On this page and the two that follow are three rooms—a living room, a dining room, and a bedroom—whose personalities are made vivid and distinctive by the use of fabric in decorating. On the fourth page of this color section are three closeups showing how fabric patterned with striking graphics can add a dramatic accent to a decorative scheme.

The charmingly traditional living room shown here has the built-in advantages of a fireplace and a beamed ceiling. The blue-and-yellow pattern fabric used on the walls and ceilings blends them into a harmonious unit and adds more warmth to the room. The same motif, used on the sofa, highlights the room with further color.

Step-by-step instructions for applying fabric to walls and ceilings are on pages 32–67. For ideas and instructions for covering furnishings, see pages 141–144, 153–155, and 206–212.

This bedroom glows with the sunshine colors of the fabric used for the walls, ceiling, and furnishings. The gathered valance and gathered tieback drapes provide an elegant treatment for the French doors, and the wrapped and stapled chair seat and the round tablecloth complement the purchased bed covering.

For ideas and step-by-step instructions for valances, drapes, and other window treatments, see pages 75–94; for table fabric ideas see pages 176–182; for chair seats and other coverings for furnishings see pages 141–144.

The rich blue background of the fabric used on the window walls of this dining room picks up the blue of the fireplace wall. The pinch-pleated drapes over Roman shades add interest to the windows, and the wrapped and stapled chair seats are an extra custom-decorated touch.

For pleated drapery instructions see pages 87–94; for chair seats see pages 141–144. Instructions for Roman shades and many other variations of roller shades begin on page 113. This combination of drapes and Roman shades is just one of many that you can devise to create striking window treatments in your home.

Top: The fabric used for the stretcher bar art and bedspread gives this room a striking, contemporary look. See pages 145–148 for stretcher bar art and other wall hanging instructions; for box-style bedspread see pages 185–187.

Bottom Left: This red and white Roman shade with buckram valance brightens up the whole window area. See pages 113–119 for instructions. Bottom Right: Striped roller shades and bedspread complement each other here. See pages 95–113 for shade instructions and pages 183–189 for spread ideas.

through. To mark the location of screw holes for drapery rods or other objects, put a short piece of broken matchstick in the hole. Cover over as just described and slit the fabric for access to the hole. Remove the matchstick.

Switches and Wall Plugs

Turn off the electricity. Remove cover plate. Clip and trim fabric to fit as illustrated.

   If you want to cover wall plates to match the background, cut a piece of fabric to match the area on the wall. Hold the switch plate and the fabric in front of the wall to align the design. Glue the fabric to the plate after cutting and wrapping as shown.

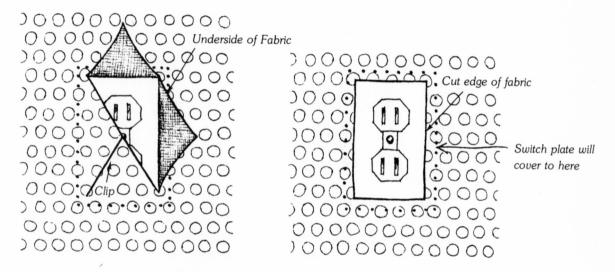

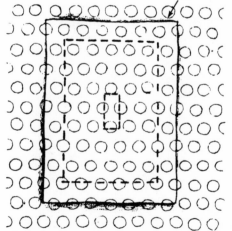

Align fabric for switch plate to design on wall where switch is

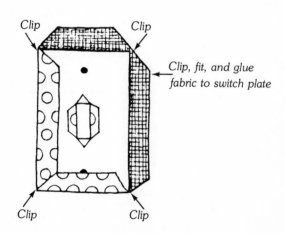

CORNERS

Trimming corners at ceiling and baseboards will be easier if you make vertical clips in the fabric as you apply it. When it is completely dry, trim it with a razor blade, cutting off two separate pieces.

For outside exposed corners trim ⅛ to ¼ inch from the corner to prevent raveling or peeling. Use a selvage edge if possible.

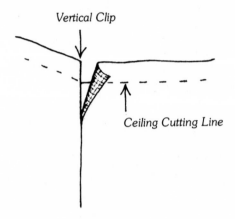

Vertical Clip

Ceiling Cutting Line

SLANTED WALLS

Dormer rooms with slanted walls can present special problems. Smaller all-over fabric designs will be easiest to work with because some mismatching is inevitable and it will be least noticeable on these designs. Be sure to allow several extra yards of fabric for rooms with slanted walls. Here is one way to handle the slanted wall problem.

1. Hang the fabric on the vertical wall first, wrapping it just around the corner about 1 inch. Slash and trim as shown.

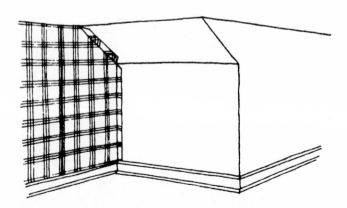

2. Apply vertical strips next to the slanted wall and the knee wall. This may require cutting into a panel of fabric to achieve a match with the adjacent wall. Wrap 1 inch of fabric around onto the next walls, slashing and trimming so that the fabric lies flat.

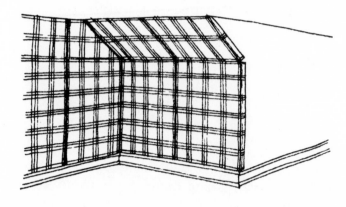

3. Next, hang vertical strips matching the knee wall, ignoring the slanted section for the moment. Fabric the triangle last. There will be a mismatch at the slant.

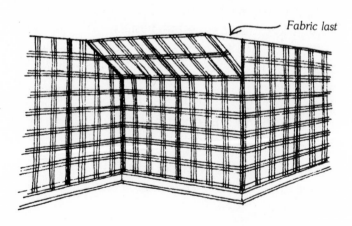

Fabric last

THREE

WINDOW TREATMENTS

Window treatments are highly effective decorating tools. You can play attractive windows up with strong contrast, or blend awkward windows into a fabric-covered wall with matching fabric. You can change apparent height and size of windows with the placement of curtains or draperies, cornices and valances, using extender plates and special rods or hardware. The style of your home and furnishings should guide the types of window treatments you will choose. Consider also the amount of privacy, light, or view that is important in the room.

Fabric choices for window treatments are varied, but must be given careful consideration. Knowing some of the general characteristics of fibers commonly used for window treatments will help, too.

Acetates: have a silk-like hand and good draping qualities. Resistant to moths and mildew. Moderate cost.

Acrylics: are light and bulky with the feel of wool. They hold pleats and are resistant to wrinkling. Dye well. Heat can cause yellowing.

Cotton: Takes dyes easily and well. Retains color. Wears well but wrinkles easily unless treated. Eventually disintegrates under strong sun.

Glass: Is an extremely strong, durable fiber. Resistant to wear, sun, water. Flame-proof. Can be abrasive. Fine glass fibers can be allergenic to some people.

Linen: has natural body and crispness. Has beautiful natural textural qualities. Does not dye well. Very prone to wrinkling.

Modacrylics: have soft hand like acrylics. Chemical resistant. Nonflammable, but has poor heat resistance. When blended with cotton has a cashmere-like hand.

Nylon: Is an extremely strong fiber. Washes and dries easily. Pleats can be heat-set. Resists mildew, moths, and wrinkling. Tends to yellow and can absorb surrounding colors.

Polyesters: are not quite as strong as nylon, but otherwise very similar in characteristics. Can be made very silk-like.

Rayon: has characteristics similar to cotton. High elastic recovery and dimensional stability. Can be washed and ironed, but tends to yellow and become fragile with time.

Silk: Luxurious, with natural luster and fine hand. Wears well. Expensive.

Blends: Rayon-acetate, rayon-cotton-polyester, cotton-polyester, etc., are often combined to give the best characteristics of the two or more fibers used.

Temperature and humidity changes and cleaning can cause fabrics to shrink or stretch. How much depends on the particular fabric and the weave. Double hemming helps keep this problem to a minimum. Although drapes and sheers may be *called* "washable" if they are pleated, think twice about washing them. Pleated headings of crinoline or buckram stiffeners often wilt in water or are otherwise affected. Draperies should be dry cleaned unless you are sure all components are washable.

The life expectancy of a drapery or window fabric depends on more than just the size and type of fiber used. How long a fabric will last depends on many factors. What is the exposure? Is there smog? What is the average temperature? Humidity? Are there children or pets in the house? What type of heating does the house have? Do you use the fireplace often? These factors and others affect the deterioration of the fibers and the life expectancy of a fabric.

To make any window treatment more successful, select and install hardware before taking measurements. Then measure each window separately. Even though they look the same, often they are not. Be sure to write down all measurements with notations as necessary. (Specific types of hardware covered later in this chapter.)

Window Types

Be creative and investigative when combining window types and treatments. Those shown here in the diagrams are meant as ideas and basic guidelines only. Research pays, for you may find or develop a really unusual window treatment.

PICTURE WINDOW

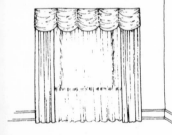

PICTURE WINDOWS

These large windows may be all one pane, a combination type with fixed center sash and casement sides, or a series of many small fixed panes. When they frame a view, you will want to be able to completely open your window treatment. The whole window may be treated as one, or as separate windows for roller and Roman shades. Cornices and valences can conceal hardware and add unity to divided treatments. Stationary side drape panels can combine effectively with roller or Roman shades or café curtains.

SLIDING GLASS DOOR

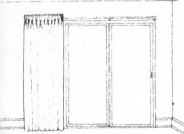

SLIDING GLASS DOORS

Usually one panel is fixed and one is movable. They are sometimes part of a glass wall, or set alone where they then serve as a large window, too. Generally, a simple treatment is best. Whatever the treatment, it should not interfere with the functioning of the door. One-way or two-way draw drapes are a natural for sliding doors. Roller and Roman shades often with stationary side panels may also be used.

DOUBLE-HUNG WINDOWS

Among the most common windows, they usually have two sashes that move up and down. Double-hung windows may be handled in many ways to create a formal or informal mood. You can add height and/or width with cornices and valances. Create a floor-length look with cafés, side panels, or folding screens. If windows are tall and narrow you can play up the proportion with cornice or valance kept narrow, too, or add width while still emphasizing height.

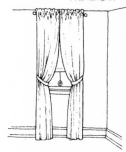

NARROW DOUBLE-HUNG WINDOW

CASEMENT WINDOWS

These windows open outward by means of a handle or crank. Their treatment should not interfere with handles, cranks, or the functioning of the window. If your casements open inward, consider draw drapes that stack back out of the way, sheers on sash rods attached to the frame, or side mounted brackets that swing aside to allow for the window.

CASEMENT WINDOW

DOOR WINDOWS

French doors and half-length windows on kitchen doors can be treated similarly. Casement curtains on sash rods are a simple answer. Roller or Roman shades may also be used. The roller is mounted in a conventional roll, usually combined with a small cornice or valance.

DOOR WINDOW

RANCH WINDOWS

These are short wide windows, usually high on the wall. They can be camouflaged or blended into a fabric wall print. Combine sill to floor cafés with draw drapes, or stationary side panels with roller or Roman shades. Cornices or valances can add still more height.

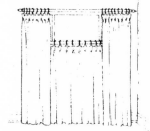

RANCH WINDOW

BASEMENT WINDOW

BASEMENT WINDOWS

These high small windows often need special attention. They are similar to ranch windows, but their smaller size calls for a treatment to add width. Consider side panels, folding screens, or fabric trim all around. If there is no room for roller brackets or Roman shades in the frame, try a ceiling mount.

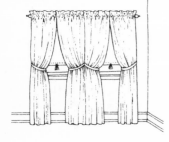

DOUBLE WINDOWS

DOUBLE AND MULTIPLE WINDOWS

These are identical-size windows that may be side by side, frames touching, or with an amount of wall space between. They are often treated as one, or they may be blended into the wall treatment and handled separately. They are forerunners of picture windows and are often found in older homes.

CORNER WINDOWS

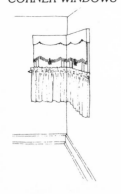

CORNER WINDOWS

Windows of this type meet or almost meet at a corner. They are usually the same height, but their widths may differ. If you want as much light as possible, consider one-way draw drapes that open from the corners back. If light is less a consideration, and if you have some wall space at the corner, curtains that pull from the center may be used. Treating the windows as a unit is a good idea. A cornice can conceal the fact that curtains or shades have been set at different heights to keep brackets from interfering with one another. For cafés or curtains, consider a special corner curtain rod.

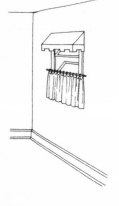

AWNING WINDOWS

AWNING WINDOWS

These consist of one or more panes that open outward and are operated by a crank or handle. Choose a treatment that plays up their architectural features and doesn't restrict air flow or operation. A canopy cornice using a standard extension rod and canopy rod can create an unusual top effect. Multiple-panel awning windows often don't have room for brackets on or in the frame, so a wall or ceiling mount may be necessary.

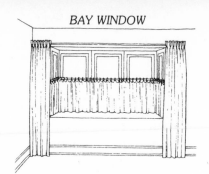

BAY WINDOW

BAY AND BOW WINDOWS

Bays have three or more windows that angle out from a room. Bows are a smooth sweeping curve of many panes that do the same. If the depth of a bay or bow window is slight, the treatment may be flat across the front. Deeper windows may be treated individually or as one with special rods and accessories. A valance on the wall above often helps unify a treatment.

DORMER WINDOWS

DORMER WINDOW

Usually deeply recessed, dormers sometimes require spring tension rods for cafés or curtains, or inside or ceiling brackets for roller shades. Treating window and walls as a single unit in a single color or print makes dormers seem less tunnel-like. Wider dormers create fewer decorating problems.

SKYLIGHTS

SKYLIGHT

These window types may be fitted with special installations of horizontally or slanting mount roller shades. Flat-panel Roman shades can be installed with the dowels resting on rails at the sides of the window. Casements on sash rods may also be used.

CATHEDRAL WINDOW

CATHEDRAL

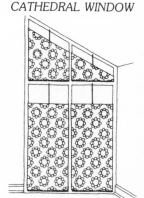

Slanted top windows can be handled with bottoms-up roller shades or shirred casements, or left uncovered. Top down or bottom-up shades may be used on the lower windows, too. Drapes on lower windows can be one- or two-way draw.

AIR CONDITIONERS

Obviously not a window type, an air conditioner in a window

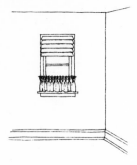

can create special decorating problems. Here are two suggestions. (1) An apron-length sheer with deep hems in a print fabric conceals the air conditioner when pulled. (2) Short cafés conceal the air conditioner, and Roman or roller shade covers top of window. To add width try draw drapes, stationary side panels, or folding screens at the sides.

Café Curtains, Shirred Curtains and Drapes, Pleated Drapes

These three window treatments are among the most popular styles. They may vary in length, heading, or fabric to suit individual needs, but general techniques in measuring, yardage estimating, and fabric preparation are common to each. The most common basic hardware types for these window treatments are listed here. (These are only a few of the many rods and accessories that are available to solve specific window problems.)

Curtain and Drapery Rods
- Standard adjustable extension rod
  Used with stationary or café curtains.
- Double adjustable extension rod
  For multiple layers, valances, crisscross styles.
- Sash and door rod
  Holds sheer casement curtains close to frame.
- Canopy rod
  For canopy valance effects with extension rod.
- Spring tension rod
  Holds curtains between two surfaces. Needs no fixtures.
- Swinging extension rod
  Used with inward opening casement windows and doors.
- Standard traverse rod
  Available in two-way or one-way draw in many styles.
- Decorative traverse rod
  Available in two-way and one-way draw in many styles.
- Wood pole and supports
  Often used with wood rings or alone. Manual pull.

- Café rods
  Available in many thicknesses and finishes. Use with all types of headings.

Clips, Hooks, and Rings
- Hooks for oval rod and for traverse rod
- Hooks for pleater tape
- Café curtain hooks, clips, and rings

Measuring
After the hardware is installed you are ready to determine yardage requirements for your window treatments. You will be working from two basic measurements.

Finished Width
The distance between the outer edges of the brackets plus the returns plus the overlap is the finished width.

Note: Return is the distance the rod projects from the wall; the *overlap* is where two panels meet and overlap at center of rod.

For Standard Rods: Measure end to end plus the returns plus the overlaps.

For Decorative Rods: Measure from just outside brackets plus return plus overlaps.

For Wood Pole Rods: Measure between brackets. Overlaps are optional.

Finished Length

The distance from the top finished edge of a panel to the bottom finished hem edge is the finished length. This length will be influenced by the type of rod or heading and whether the curtain stops at the sill, apron, or floor length. If you do not have an apron on your windows, the curtain may stop 4 inches below the sill.

Estimating Yardage

Step One: Determining Total Fabric Width

To obtain the necessary fullness (double, two and a half times, or triple) for pleating and gathering each panel, it is often necessary to seam several full widths and part widths together. (The diagram illustrates a two-panel window treatment. You will need one panel for one-way draw or stationary curtains.)

Finished Width (Rod, Returns, Overlap)
x Fullness + Side Hems + Seam Allowances
_____

= Total Width Needed

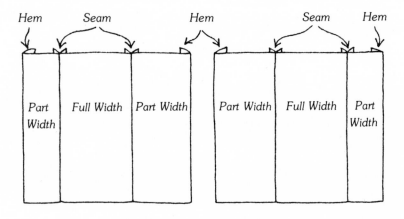

Hem   Seam   Hem   Seam   Hem

Part Width | Full Width | Part Width   Part Width | Full Width | Part Width

To obtain the necessary length for each panel you will have to take into account headings, hems, and the pattern match.

A. For plain fabrics or fabrics not requiring pattern match:

_____'' Heading or Casing

+ _____'' Finished Length

+ _____'' Bottom Double Hem
_____

= _____'' Cut Length for Each Width and Part Width

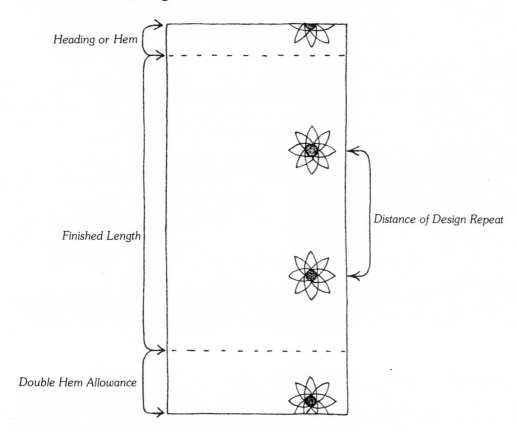

Heading or Hem

Finished Length

Distance of Design Repeat

Double Hem Allowance

B. For fabrics with a pattern repeat figure length. Divide the result in inches by the size of the pattern repeats. If this results in a fraction, order enough extra fabric to get an additional repeat. Most repeats are from 12 to 24 inches. Extra fabric can be used for pillows, placemats, and other accessories.

For example, if the cut length A is 97 inches and the pattern repeat is 12 inches:

Length needed, including hems = 97 inches
Pattern repeat   = 12 inches
Divide 97 by 12   = 8.1
Number of repeats needed   = 9
No. of repeats X size of repeats = 108 inches
Total Cut Length per Width

Step Three: Converting Panel Lengths and Widths to Yards

_____'' Total Cut Length (from A or B)

x _____No. of Fabric Widths Needed

= _____'' Total Inches of Fabric Needed ÷ 36 inches = Total Yards Needed

Cutting and Preparing the Fabric Panels

Straightening Fabric

In order for them to hang straight and smooth, curtains and drapes must be cut on the true lengthwise and crosswise grain of the fabric.

Matching and Placement of Design

Besides matching a patterned fabric at the seams, the design motifs should be placed so the effect will be most pleasing to the eye. It would be ideal to have complete motifs near both the top and bottom of the panel. When this is not possible, try to position a complete motif near the top on long draperies where it will be more noticeable, and on the bottom on short curtains or drapes. Be sure that motifs are positioned to match on each pair of panels, and on all windows in the same room.

CAFÉ CURTAINS

The endless variations possible with café curtains make them one of the most popular window treatments. While they may have any style top heading (pleats, scallops, gathers), their common characteristic is that they cover the window in sections rather than in one piece as regular curtains do. Mounted alone, with valance, cornice, or roller shade, or in tiers, cafés can be easily adjusted to let in light through the upper portion of a window while maintaining privacy below. Nearly any fabric type works for café curtains, as long as it fits the mood and style of the room. Although cafés need not be lined, lining them is advisable if they will be exposed to the sun for long periods of time.

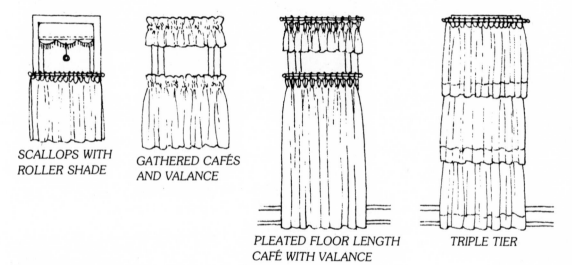

*SCALLOPS WITH
ROLLER SHADE*

*GATHERED CAFÉS
AND VALANCE*

*PLEATED FLOOR LENGTH
CAFÉ WITH VALANCE*

TRIPLE TIER

Measuring

The top café curtain rod is usually mounted on top of the window frame or on the wall just above the frame. The second rod is placed on the frame at the center. For some styles the window is divided into more sections.

For café curtains, the finished length is the distance from the rod to the bottom edge of the curtain for ring and clip-on styles, and from above the rod to bottom for pleated and shirred styles. For tiered curtains add a 3-inch overlap. The finished width is described and illustrated on page 75.

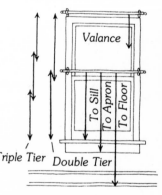

Valance

To Sill *To Apron* *To Floor*

Triple Tier *Double Tier*

Determining Yardage

Use the steps outlined in "Estimating Yardage" to determine final yardage, using the following allowances.

Length:

Top Hems	Straight hem with clip-on rings	2 inches
	Gathered casing and heading	3 inches
	Scallops	2 inches plus depth of scallops
	Pleats	4 to 5 inches
Bottom Hems		4 to 6 inches for double hems

Width

Side Hems	4 inches per panel (for double 2-inch hems)
Seams	Use standard ½'' seam allowance (French seams for sheers)
Fullness	Double or 2½X for medium or heavy fabrics, Triple for sheers

Construction of Café Curtains

Plain Hems with Clip-on Hooks or Rings

1. Cut and seam the café panels. Turn, press, and stitch double 1-inch side hems, then a 1-inch double top hem and a 3- or 4-inch double bottom hem.

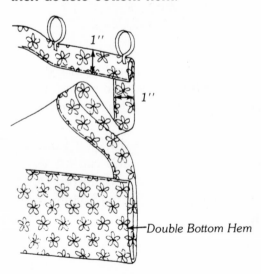

1''

1''

Double Bottom Hem

Gathered Casing and Heading

1. Cut and seam the café panels. Turn, press, and stitch double 1-inch side hems and a double 3 or 4-inch bottom hem.

2. Turn down ½ inch then 2½ inches to form the top hem. Stitch the folded edge; then pin fit the curtain to the rod to determine the depth of the casing and the amount of heading desired. Stitch the casing, using pins as a guide. Allow enough ease so fabric gathers easily.

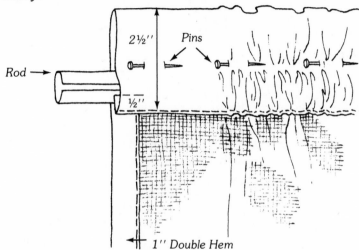

Scallops

1. Determine the depth of the scallops. Cut and seam the café panels. Turn, press, and stitch double 1-inch side hems.

2. Cut a strip of paper the width of the finished panel and 8 to 10 inches deep. Using a saucer or small bowl about 4 to 6 inches in diameter, start at the center and draw half circles 2 inches from the bottom and allowing 1½ inch between scallops.

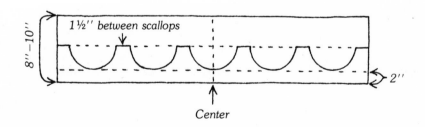

3. Fold the top of the curtain down the depth of the paper pattern from the top of the scallops to the bottom edge. Center the pattern on the panel. Pin and trace the scallops. Stitch the scallops. Then cut out each one leaving ¼-inch seam allowance. Clip the seam allowance, being careful not to cut into the stitching.

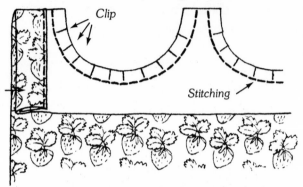

4. Turn the heading right side out and press. Press and stitch a ¼-inch hem along the raw edge. Stitch or fuse the side edge of the heading into place. Add clip-on or sew-on rings of each scallop.

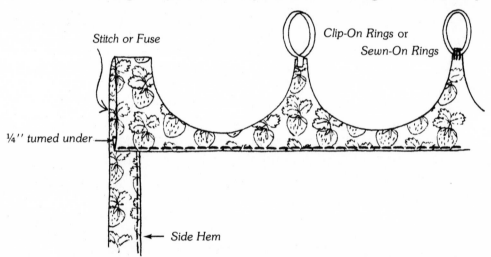

5. Turn, press, and stitch a double 3- or 4-inch bottom hem.

Pleats

Follow the directions for pleated drapes, adjusting the length as necessary for café style. Do not allow for overlap or return unless you are using a traverse rod or one with side returns.

SHIRRED CURTAINS AND DRAPES

Shirred curtains often are constructed of sheer fabrics, although this is not necessary for special effects or drapery styles. They may be used alone or in sheer fabric under draperies, short and ruffled for an early American effect, shirred onto wooden poles for easy-to-sew draperies, or gathered onto rods at both top and bottom as casement curtains.

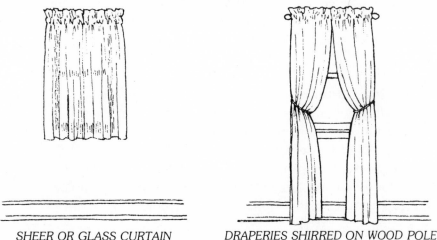

SHEER OR GLASS CURTAIN   *DRAPERIES SHIRRED ON WOOD POLE*

Measuring

Rods for shirred curtains are usually mounted on the outer corners of the window frame. Drapery pole brackets may be mounted just beside the window as preferred. The finished length is from the top of the heading to the bottom hem. The finished width is the distance between brackets on the poles, rod plus returns for standard rods.

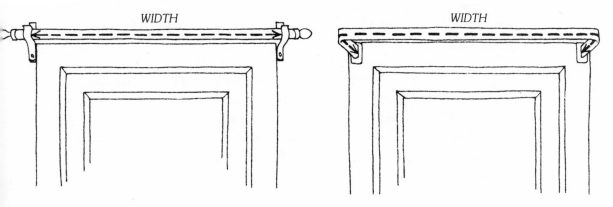

Determining Yardage

Use the steps outlined earlier in this chapter to determine final yardage, using the following allowances.

Length	For sheers	Finished length plus 9 inches
	For drapes	Finished length plus 13 inches
	For casements	Finished length plus 6 inches
Width	Side hems	4 inches per panel
	Seams	Use standard ½ inch seam allowance
	Fullness:	Triple for sheers
		Double or 2½ for medium to heavy fabrics

Shirred Curtains

Plain Shirred Curtains

Follow the directions for gathered casing and heading café curtains (p. 81) for use with standard rods. If you are using a wood pole drapery rod through the casing, remember to allow for an extra-long heading to accommodate the size of the pole. To form the top hem, turn the fabric down ½ inch, then 4½ inches.

Casement Curtains

Follow the general instructions for gathered casing and heading café-curtains, but measure for and sew an identical heading at the top and bottom for shirring onto sash rods.

Shirred Lined Draperies

These draperies are extremely attractive gathered on wooden pole rods. The heading gives a decorative touch. Draperies in this style may be left unlined if you prefer. (In that case, follow directions for "Plain Shirred Curtains.") However, lining adds body, protection, and a custom touch.

1. Cut and seam the panel lengths. Be sure to allow for pattern match. Cut the lining 14 inches shorter and 3 inches narrower than the drapery fabric. Seam the lining and press.

2. Turn, press, and stitch a 4-inch double hem in the drapery fabric and a 2-inch double hem in the lining fabric.

3. Turn and press 5 inches of fabric toward the right side on the drapery top.

4. Center the lining on the right side of the drapery at the top edges. (The drapery will extend 1½ inches on each side of the lining.) Pin and stitch a ½-inch seam. Press the seam allowance up.

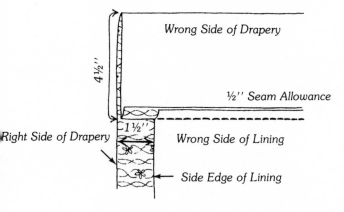

5. Slide the edges of the lining over so they are even with the side edges of the drapery. Pin them in place and stitch with ½-inch seams.

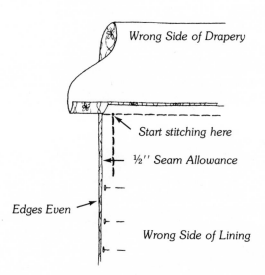

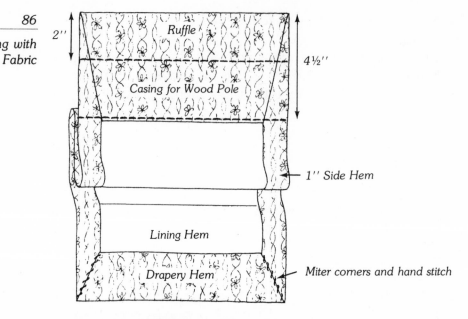

6. Turn the drapery right side out. Press, centering the lining so that 1-inch hems are visible on each side. Stitch across the top of the drapery 4½ inches from the top folded edge. Stitch again 2 inches from the top edge. Fold the bottom side seams into a miter and tack them in place.

7. Make tie backs by cutting a strip of fabric approximately 7 inches wide and the desired length. (To determine the width and length hang the drapery in the window and pull it back with a strip of fabric until the desired effect is achieved. Measure the length needed and add seam allowances.) Seam the long edges. If desired, add a strip of iron-on interfacing for body, or cut a strip of drapery stiffener and fuse it in place. Turn the tie back right side out and press it.

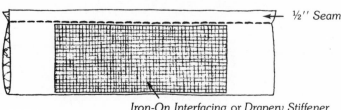

Iron-On Interfacing or *Drapery Stiffener*

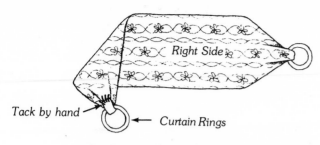

Tack by hand

Right Side

Curtain Rings

8. Turn raw ends inside and stitch them. Fold both ends to a point and tack them to plastic or metal curtain rings. Anchor the tie backs to hooks fastened to the outside of the window frame.

PLEATED DRAPES

Draperies are perhaps the most favored window treatment. Often they are used alone but may be most effective when combined with curtains, shades, valances, and other window treatments. Use them to change mood, apparent size of windows or wall spaces, or to block or admit light. They can affect the look and appearance of the outside of the house, too, so consider this when you select fabric and decide whether to use a lining.

Measuring

Traverse rods are usually installed on the wall at the sides of the window frame, with decorative rods 1 inch above the frame, and conventional rods 2 inches above the frame. (They should be approximately 4 inches above the glass.)

The finished length is the distance from the bottom of the rings on decorative rods or ½ inch above a standard rod to the bottom of the finished hem. The finished width is based on the length of the rod plus returns and center overlap.

The rod length is determined by the width of the glass and the stackback needed. *Stackback* is the area covered by the draperies when they are open, allowing them to uncover all of the glass. If your drapes are two-way draw, half goes on each side of the window. For one-way draw the stackback is all on one side.

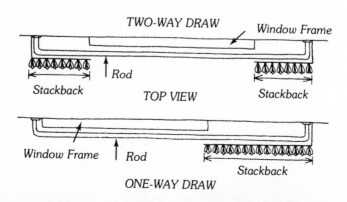

TWO-WAY DRAW Window Frame

Rod

Stackback TOP VIEW Stackback

Window Frame Rod

Stackback

ONE-WAY DRAW

Determining Yardage

Using the steps outlined earlier in this chapter, determine the final yardage with the following allowances:

Length:

Lined drapes	Finished length plus 8½ inches
Lining	Cut 5½ inches shorter than drapery fabric
Unlined drapes with 4 inch stiffener	Finished length plus 12½ inches
Unlined drapes with pleater tape	Finished length plus 8½ inches

Width:

Side Hems	Add 4 inches per panel
Lining	Cut 6 inches narrower than drapery fabric
Fullness	Allow double, 2½X or triple depending on fabric
Seams	Use standard ½-inch seam allowance

Construction of Pleated Drapes

Lined Drapes with Stiffener

1. Cut, seam, and press drapery panel widths and lining widths. Make a double 4-inch hem in the drapery and a double 2-inch hem in the lining.

2. Position the lining and drapery, right sides together. Match the top and side edges. The lining hem will be 1½ inches above the drapery hem. Stitch ½-inch side seams.

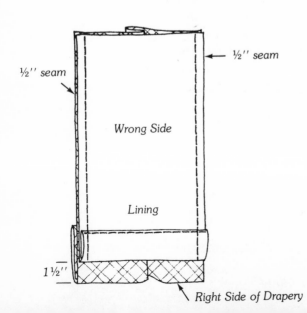

½'' seam

½'' seam

Wrong Side

Lining

1½''

Right Side of Drapery

3. Center the lining on the drapery fabric and press the seams toward the lining. Stitch the top edge with a ½-inch seam allowance.

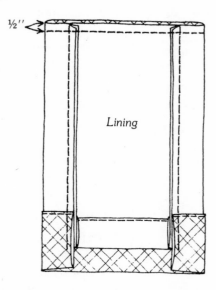

½''

Lining

4. Place the stiffener on the seam allowance as shown. Stitch in place. Turn the entire panel right side out like a pillowcase. (The stiffener will be entirely enclosed.) Press.

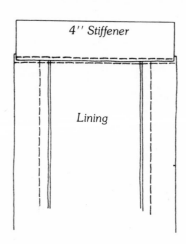

4'' Stiffener

Lining

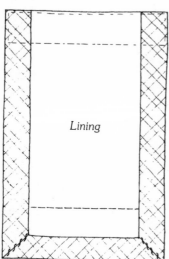

Lining

5. Follow the directions given later in this chapter for spacing the pleats and "Finishing Touches" (p. 94) to prepare drapes for hanging.

Lined Drapes with Pleater Tape

1. Follow steps one and two for lined drapes with stiffener.

2. Turn the panel inside out like a pillowcase. Center the lining and press it with the seam allowances toward the lining.

3. Baste the top drapery and lining edges together ⅜ inch from the raw edge. Turn the pleater tape ends under ½ inch. Lay the top edge of the pleater tape next to the basting stitches on the right side of the drapery, and stitch it in place. (Align pockets on the tape so the pleats fall on the corners of the rod.)

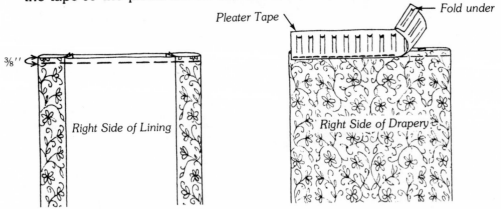

4. Turn the pleater tape to the wrong side of the drapery. Press. Stitch the bottom edge of the tape, being careful not to stitch the pockets closed. Tack or fuse the edges of the pleater tape.

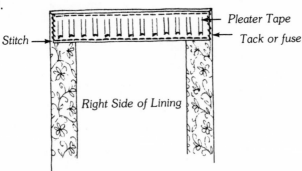

5. Insert pleater hooks and hang the draperies. See "Finishing Touches."

1. Cut, seam, and press the panel widths. Make a 4-inch double bottom hem. Place a 4-inch wide stiffener on the wrong side of the drapery fabric ½ inch from the top edge and 2 inches from the side edges. Stitch the lower edge of the stiffener. Turn the top edge of the drapery fabric over the stiffener and press.

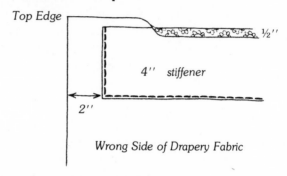

2. Fold the stiffener toward the wrong side of the fabric forming a top hem. Stitch through all of the thicknesses along the bottom edge of the stiffened heading. Trim the side seam as illustrated, and fold in the side seam, mitering at the top. Fasten the side seams by hand, by machine, or by fusing.

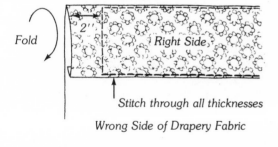

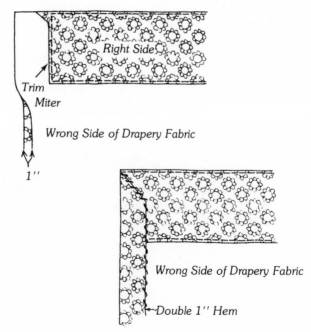

3. Finish the bottom side edge by folding a miter and tacking it in place.

4. For position and stitching of pleats see "Spacing the Pleats" and "Finishing Touches."

Unlined Drapes with Pleater Tape

1. Cut, seam, and press the panel widths. Turn the top of the drapery fabric down ½ inch and press it. Position the pleater tape ¼ inch from the top edge and 2 inches from the side edge, with the pockets in position so that the first pleat will fall at the corner of the rod. Stitch the tape in place across the top, then across the bottom. Be careful not to stitch the pockets closed.

2. Fold and stitch a double 4-inch bottom hem.

3. Fold and press double 1-inch side hems. Slipstitch, machine stitch, or fuse the side hems. Miter the bottom corner.

4. Insert pleater hooks and hang the drapes. See "Finishing Touches."

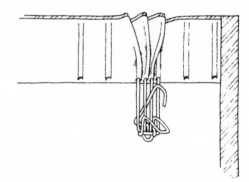

Spacing the Pleats

The top edge of the panel must be pleated to fit the rod.

1. To determine how much fabric must be taken up in pleats:

A. _____'' Total width of panel

   – _____'' Minus finished width (rod length, returns, overlaps)

   = _____'' Total inches to be pleated

B. _____'' Total inches to be pleated ÷ 4 to 5 inches to determine the number of pleats * = _____ Total No. of pleats required

*An uneven number of pleats is always preferred so adjust the number from 4 to 5 to obtain an uneven number.

2. Mark off returns and overlaps on each panel. (If there are none, leave 2 inches on each end.) For two-way draw drapes, the return is generally longer than the overlap. Then mark off the pleat depth (4 to 5 inches) at the sides next to the returns. The next pleat is next to the overlaps. Then divide the panel in half by bringing pins together to center the third pleat. The fourth pleat is determined by bringing pleats 1 and 3 together, and so on.

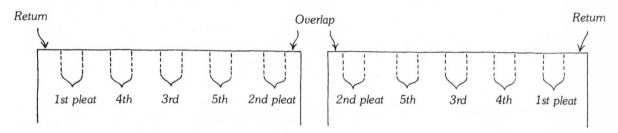

3. Form individual pleats by bringing each pair of markings together and pinning. Remeasure the coverage obtained to be sure it agrees with the finished width. Adjust if necessary.

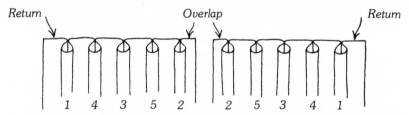

4. Stitch from the top edge to ¾ inch below the heading. Backtack securely. Divide the fullness into thirds. Pin and stitch by hand or machine. Press the pleats above the stitching.

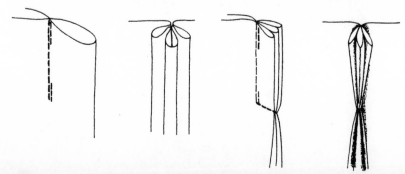

Finishing Touches

Drapery Weights

Draperies and curtains, particularly full-length styles, hang better if weights are used at the lower edges. Weights are available in several shapes, covered and uncovered. It is advisable to enclose them in the hem when possible. They also may be covered with a bit of leftover drapery fabric and stitched to the side seam allowance at the hem. Weighted tapes are often used in the hems of sheer curtains to help keep them from billowing. Insert the tape in the hem, cut to fit. Tack at the hem near the side edges. Remove for laundering.

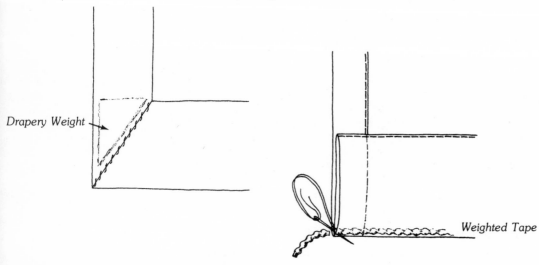

Drapery Weight

Weighted Tape

Anchors

If the outside side edges of the drapes do not remain straight and taut, drapery anchors are available to hold them in line. You may also use small cup hooks fastened to the wall behind plastic rings sewn to the drapery hem.

Setting Pleats

Train the folds in your drapes by opening them and arranging the folds evenly from top to bottom. Tie them loosely with several strips of fabric or soft cords and leave them for several days. Drapery sprays to help set the folds while they are bundled are available at drapery shops.

Roller Shades

Roller shades are versatile, energy-saving, attractive window accents. Used on very sunny windows, roller shapes protect fabrics and finishes and admit 50 percent less heat than a bare window. They may be used alone or combined with other window treatments. In addition to their use at windows roller shades can replace cupboard or closet doors, hide shelves and storage areas, and also serve as room dividers. Knowing a few basic terms can be helpful in making your own shades.

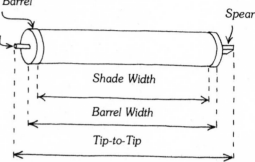

If you wish to cut a roller down to a specific window size, remove the pin with pliers and pull off the metal cap. Saw the roller to size, replace the cap, and hammer the pin into place. Be sure the pin goes in straight. Shortening a roller is always done from the pin end to avoid disturbing the roller spring mechanism. For installation purposes, rollers are always measured from tip to tip.

Shades are hung at the window in one of two ways—conventional roll or reverse roll.

A conventional roll shade fits closer to the window, thus preventing light streaks along the edges. The roller shows unless a cornice or valance is used.

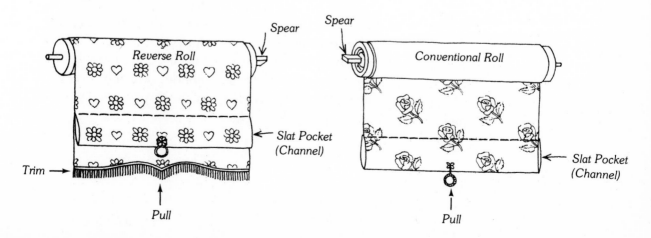

For a reverse roll shade, the spear (flat end) should be on your right when the fabric side of the shade faces you. In reverse roll the shade cloth is in front of the roller, so the shade sits out from the window. This method avoids handles or projections and the roller doesn't show, but streaks of light are more likely along edges of the shade.

WHERE TO GET ROLLERS

Bare standard rollers and heavy-duty rollers can be purchased cut to fit in shade shops and often in hardware or variety stores. You can also purchase inexpensive ready-made shades and remove the plastic and use its roller and slat. (The only danger is that the inexpensive roller may not have a spring of good enough quality to lift the weight of a fabric shade.) If you choose this method, use the plastic shade for a pattern. When you purchase a bare roller, the slat should be included. Slats need about a 1¼-inch tuck that can be on the front or back side of the shade. The channel or hem for the slat should be at least 2 inches above the top of the decorative edge, if one is used.

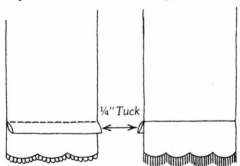

The width of the window is related to the size of the roller diameter. As a shade gets wider, the diameter of the roller increases to assure strength and resistance to sagging. If your shade will be heavier than average, as in a laminated shade, you may wish to select a larger diameter or heavy-duty roller. A very long shade might also require a heavy-duty roller.

SPRING TENSION

Do not twist or attempt to adjust the spear (mechanism end) when the roller is not in its brackets. To adjust a too tight or too loose spring, see "Easy Care and Upkeep." However, if a spear should get bumped and the tension is released on the spring, probably you have disengaged the teeth from the notch (see spearlining diagram). To rewind the spring slip the spear through the tines of a fork, and holding the roller firmly rotate the fork several revolutions. You will feel the spring become tighter and harder to turn. *Take care not to overwind or you can break the spring.* Tilt the roller so the teeth catch in the spear notch, and lock the spring in place.

SPEARLINING

When you wish shades on side-by-side windows to stop at the same level automatically when raised, use a technique called spearlining before you attach shades to rollers.

1. Lay two or more bare rollers down on a piece of paper. (The paper is to protect the surface so you can draw lines with a felt-tip pen or pencil).
2. Position the rollers so the teeth which engage the notch on the end mechanism are at exactly the same location.
3. Hold the rollers firmly and draw a line on the first roller. Set it aside and draw a line on the second roller, and so on. The guide lines you have just drawn are now "synchronized."

Teeth in same position

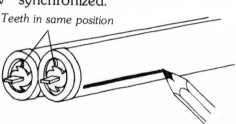

Felt Pen or Pencil

4. Attach shades to the rollers along the guide lines.
5. Place in brackets of windows. The shades will now stop evenly side by side.

MEASURING

Accuracy in measuring is very important. An inaccuracy of even ¼ inch can prevent smooth action and fit. When measuring for shades, use a wood rule or metal tape; cloth tape measures or strings can stretch. Windows may look the same size, but they seldom are. Frames can vary from top to bottom and from one window to another. Be sure to measure each window separately at the point where the brackets will be installed. If you prefer, install brackets first and then measure for roller length.

Width

Mark the position where the brackets are to be installed. Be sure the marks, and hence the brackets, are level or the shade may not roll.

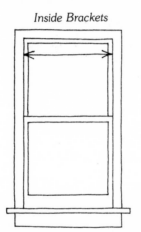

Inside Brackets

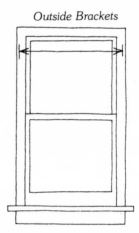

Outside Brackets

Measure from one inside surface of the window frame to the opposite inside surface. If your roller is being cut out for you, indicate this is tip-to-tip measurement for an inside bracket mount (IBM); thus the dealer will automatically subtract ⅛ inch for clearance in the window. If the brackets are already mounted and you are cutting your own roller, be sure to measure "wood-to-wood" and subtract ⅛ inch to obtain the tip-to-tip measurement.

Mark the position of the brackets on the trim or wall and measure the distance between them. Mount brackets so there will be 1½ to 2 inches of overlap on the window frame. This helps prevent light streaks along the sides of the shade. When measuring for outside brackets, keep in mind the difference between the foot of the bracket and the bracket itself. This can affect the fit of the roller.

Mark the position where the ceiling brackets will be placed and measure the distance between them. The shade should overlap the window frame 1½ to 2 inches. For the length, measure from the ceiling to the lower windowsill.

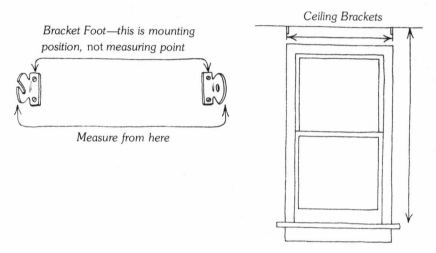

Bracket Foot—*this is mounting position,* not *measuring point*

Measure from here

Ceiling Brackets

Bottom-Up Installation

Measure the same as for inside or outside brackets, but take the measurements at the bottom of the window opening. If brackets are installed on the sill or floor, mark the position where the brackets will be positioned and measure the distance between them.

If you are replacing the entire shade, roller too, take the measurements as just described. If you are replacing only the shade cloth, measure the shade fabric if it fits and hangs well.

ROLLER SHADE BRACKETS

Standard Inside Bracket

A standard inside bracket is the most common type, and may be used wherever there is enough depth inside a windowframe to accommodate the roller. This type of bracket may be reversed— that is, you may place the spear bracket on the right frame and the round pin bracket on the left. You may also purchase a special reverse bracket.

Inside Extension Bracket (Footless Bracket)

This type is mounted inside the window frame. It requires less space than an inside bracket. It extends slightly into the room away from the window. Often it is used for narrow framed windows or to extend the shade outward to clear casement cranks, door hinges, and so on.

Ranch Bracket

This is a clear plastic version of the inside extension bracket. It is curved to follow the contour of narrow, contemporary window frames.

Sash Run (Boston) Bracket

This is a special bracket for use with all-wood, double-hung windows. It is mounted at the top of the sash run (the track where the window slides up and down), it has a "bumper" to stop the window when it is raised. The shade is mounted reverse roll to clear the window below. This results in a shade close to the glass, overlapping the frame, for an almost light-proof installation.

Outside Bracket

This bracket is mounted on the trim or wall adjacent to the window. It is used when a window is not deep enough to accommodate an inside bracket. Use outside brackets for shades wider than the window, to eliminate light streaks at the sides, or just to give the illusion of a wider window. If the brackets are mounted on the wall, an expansion bolt or anchor is recommended.

Combination Bracket

These are dual-purpose brackets that hold both a window-shade and a curtain rod, and are available in fixed or adjustable types. They eliminate the need for two sets of brackets, making a cleaner line at the window. Brackets that hold a café curtain and a roller shade are also available.

Ceiling Brackets

This type is very useful on ceiling-high windows, bow windows, or those with deep recesses. They may be installed on the ceiling itself. They give standard windows an illusion of extra height. Reverse roll is recommended unless a cornice or valance covers the roller. They are useful on an overhang above a window or on double-hung aluminum windows.

Double Brackets

Double-hung brackets are designed for two shades on the same window; usually one is translucent, the other a room-darkener. The roomside shade gets reverse roll in many cases to avoid interference with the other. They are available in outside and inside mount, or for inside installations two single brackets may be mounted one above the other.

Similar brackets can be installed at the center of the window so that one, a bottom-up shade, covers the upper sash. A regular shade pulls down to cover the lower sash, permitting both windows to be opened without causing the shades to flap. Many institutions, particularly schools, use them.

Horizontal Installation

For skylights inside or ceiling brackets may be used, depending on whether the installation is within the frame or on the face of the skylight. For very large skylights, stretched wires are used to keep the shade taut. The shade is operated by a cord and pulley system similar to those in bottom-up shades.

Bottom-Up Shades

If a shade is mounted at the bottom of a window, it pulls up by means of a pulley mechanism. This is especially effective when privacy is desired and for cathedral-type windows which require a slanting shade top to fit the window contour. Brackets for sill mounting or outside brackets are particularly adapted to bottom-up use. Special brackets may also be ordered.

THINGS TO THINK ABOUT BEFORE YOU START YOUR SHADE

Different methods can be used to create a roller shade. It is best to make a test sample of the methods you are considering. This can help you answer some questions in advance. For example:

- Is the method compatible with the fabric? Will it produce enough but not too much body? If the backing is too lightweight, the edges of the shade ripple. The shade won't have enough body to maintain its shape. Liquid stiffeners (dips) often don't "take" on fabrics treated for stain resistance.
- How long will the shade be? If it is very long, laminated methods may become too heavy or too thick to roll well without special brackets and a heavy-duty roller.
- How will the shade look from the street? If a uniform color effect is desired, a laminated method should be chosen, perhaps with a blackout backing.
- Is room darkening desired? (Only commercial black-out backings can provide complete darkening.) Some methods transmit more light than others. Hold samples up to the light to test for color changes and light transmission.
- What about sun fading? Some fading can be expected over a period of time, with unbonded methods being most susceptible. Bright and dark colors fade most.
- How much am I willing to spend? No matter what method you choose, you will be saving 40 to 60 percent (or more) of the cost of a custom-made shade.
- What is available in my area? Not all backings or stiffeners are available everywhere.

STAGE 1: GETTING READY

1. *Select shade fabric.* Firmly woven fabric is important, especially for larger shades. Looser weaves will tend to stretch and ravel more easily. Fabric may be placed on the crosswise direction, design permitting, since it will be stabilized when fused, bonded, or glued. This will allow wider shades than the normal fabric width of 45 or 54 inches and is very helpful for short, wide ranch-style windows.

2. *Assemble materials.* Roller, brackets, fabric, backing or stiffener, slat, shade, pull, trim, scissors, glue, staple gun or tape, carpenter's square, rulers, iron.

3. *Make a test sample.* Select the methods you feel will work best for your fabric and the placement of your shade. Try them according to the detailed instructions that follow under "Making the Shade." Evaluate them and make a selection.

4. *Preparing the fabric.* Spread the fabric out and inspect it. Be aware of designs that need to be centered or positioned in a particular way. Think through your plan before you cut the fabric. When you handle the fabric, be careful not to stretch or distort the edges. This is most important for bonding methods that require heat. Fabric is softer and more easily stretched when it is hot or warm. Allow fabric to cool before moving it.

5. *The work surface.* You need a large flat area so that the shade is completely supported. If the shade is hanging over the edge of an ironing board or a table, it will be difficult to keep measurements accurate, and there is danger of stretching the edges of the shade. A Ping-Pong table, a 4x8 foot piece of plywood or some tables pushed together will all work. You can also work on the floor, although it will be more difficult.

6. *Cutting the fabric to general size.* Cut the fabric slightly wider than the tip-to-tip measurement of the roller and as long as the area to be covered, plus 12 to 16 inches for roll over. Roll over is the safety margin left on the roller when the shade is pulled down. It prevents the shade from being torn from the roller when the shade is pulled. Twelve inches is standard; sixteen is allowed if a deep ornamental shaped hem is used. The shade will be cut to exact measurements later, but accuracy in cutting now saves time then.

STAGE 2: MAKING THE SHADE— CHOOSE YOUR METHOD

Commercial Iron-on or Self-Adhesive Backings

Using these backings, shade making becomes easy and your results become professional. Backings are available by the yard at shade shops and sometimes in fabric stores and drapery departments. The iron-ons come in 36, 45, and 68 inch widths in translucent and blackout versions. Wider ones are sometimes available on special order. Self-adhesive backings, usually found only in the blackout version, come in 45- or 50-inch widths.

The backings may be used with lengthwise grain running from the top of the window to the bottom or turned crosswise, with the lengthwise grain running from one side of the window to the other. They are best used crosswise, however, since the shade will roll more smoothly this way, especially in reverse roll. If heavy fabrics do create puckers in reverse, use a conventional roll and add a cornice or valance to conceal the roller.

Avoid getting ravelings between the fabric and the backing when you fuse or laminate a translucent shade. They will show through when the shade is hung in the window.

Bonding the Iron-on Backing

Cut fabric and backing to general side and mark the center top and bottom. Place the backing on the lightly padded work surface and remove the paper liner, which protects the adhesive. Set the liner aside and save. Center the fabric on top of the adhesive and smooth it in place with your hands. Using a cool dry iron, press the fabric from the center outward. Once the fabric has been pressed in place with a cool iron, turn the iron up to the fabric temperature and continue to press and assure a good smooth bond. Let the fabric cool completely. The bond sets as the fabric cools. Never touch the backing with a hot iron. If you do press on the backing side, as with heavier fabrics or when making a slat pocket, use the paper liner as a press cloth and place it on top of the backing before using the iron.

Center Marks

Commercial Backing

Center Marks

Fabric

Bonding Self-Adhesive Backing
Prepare the fabric as above, then peel off backing paper, position the fabric, and press down with a smoothing motion of your hands. Use a roller, bottle, or rolling pin to assure a tight bond. On larger shades it may be easier to roll the fabric onto the backing, smoothing as you go to prevent puckers.

Gluing to a Shade or Backing

This is a relatively easy process. Roll the glue on with a roller, then apply the fabric. You can use a good quality cloth-coated vinyl backing from a shade shop, or a roller shade you already have. (Best results will be obtained with a heavy vinyl or vinyl-coated cloth.) Although it is possible to glue to a very inexpensive plastic shade, you will usually get puckers on the back side. This is partly due to the lightweight plastic and the fact that you can't use an iron to help set and smooth the laminating process.

It is best to use commercial laminating glue, available in quart or gallon sizes through shade shops or drapery departments. These glues dry clear, tacky, and flexible. If you cannot locate a commercial glue, a craft glue may work, but be sure to test it first by pouring a small amount on a piece of fabric. If the glue dries clear and flexible, it is a possibility. Then make a sample with fabric and shade backing or high up on your roller shade. Common household white glues are usually not acceptable because they dry stiff and brittle.

Bonding with Laminating Adhesive

Cover the unpadded work surface with brown paper or heavy plastic. Masking tape all the edges of the backing, fastening one edge to the edge of the table, and using that as a guideline for a straight edge. Center the fabric over the backing, then tape the top edge in place about 1 inch above the backing.

Now carefully roll the fabric up on a tube, keeping the edge straight and even. To start, bring the fabric back over the tube until the side edges line up even. Then roll all the way to the masking tape.

Fabric Rolled on Tube

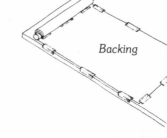

Backing

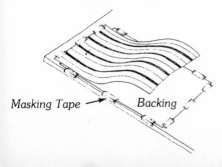

Masking Tape *Backing*

Edges Even

Edges Even

Pour the glue into a paint roller pan, then thoroughly coat a short nap roller. Roll quickly and evenly until a thin uniform coat of glue covers the backing. There must be no skips or dry areas. (If the glue is applied too thick, it may come through to the front when the fabric is pressed in place.)

Begin to roll the fabric slowly and evenly onto the backing. Smooth it with your hands as you go. Always work with stripes, not across them. With a medium-warm iron go over the whole shade slowly and evenly. This helps start the glue drying and removes air pockets, assuring a good bond. Allow the glue to dry overnight if possible (at least eight hours) before cutting and shaping.

Clean up the glue with water immediately after finishing. Glue is water soluble while wet, but permanent when dry. Wear old clothes. If you need to carry over the gluing to another day, wrap the roller in plastic and put it in the refrigerator. It will keep for more than a week this way. Glue sets faster in hot weather, so in summer try to glue in the cool of the morning.

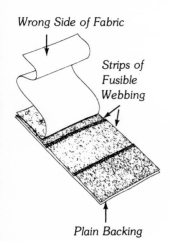

Wrong Side of Fabric

Strips of Fusible Webbing

Plain Backing

Fabric Backing and Fusible Webbing

This is a three-layer method only in the construction. It involves the heat-sensitive webbings described earlier. This method makes a durable and very attractive shade, although it takes a bit more time and patience to complete. Materials are readily available in fabric stores, and the shade will always roll well in conventional or reverse.

Make a sandwich of the face fabric and cotton sateen drapery lining (or firmly woven white fabric) with the fusible web in the middle. (Slightly overlap the webbing strips.) As with all iron-ons, position the layers carefully on a large flat surface. Start in the center and press your way out to the sides.

Be careful not to lift or pull the fabric while it is warm or push the iron hard on the surface of the fabric. This can stretch edges and cause distortion that may prevent the shade from looking attractive and hanging correctly. Steam press from both sides, allowing the fabric to cool before turning it.

Liquid Stiffeners and Aerosol Sprays

When using these products just the fabric is stiffened. There is no backing. The lack of a backing will make a thinner shade when it is rolled up, so that longer shades are possible. The color and design of the fabric will be more obvious from the outside of the house, and the shade may be more susceptible to sun fading. Liquid stiffeners and aerosols are generally used for shades that will not require splicing.

Liquid Stiffeners

A commercially made dipping solution stiffens fabric for use on roller shades and cornices. This product is found in shade shops, fabric stores, and some drapery departments. The manufacturer recommends dipping the fabric in the solution, then hanging it to dry. If you find this a bit awkward and messy, here are a couple of suggestions to simplify matters.

1. Lay the fabric out on a plastic sheet. Apply the solution with a paint roller. Allow the fabric to dry in place.
2. A second method involves hanging the fabric over a tension bar in the bathtub or suspending it from a rafter in the basement, garage, or patio. Using a good spray bottle with a pull trigger, spray the solution on both sides of the fabric. Put something underneath to catch the drips.

On occasion I have taken a piece of fabric, such as cotton duck or sailcloth, and sponged on liquid starch straight from the bottle. If a residue of starch shows on darker fabrics it can usually be wiped away with a damp sponge.

Making a test sample of your fabric will tell you if the solutions give enough body to suit you. Stain-resistant finishes on some fabrics can prevent adequate absorption of the solution.

Aerosol Spray Stiffeners

Hang the pressed fabric from a rafter or rod in a well-ventilated area and spray from both sides. When the fabric is dry and stiff, proceed with cutting and mounting. As with all methods, do a test sample first.

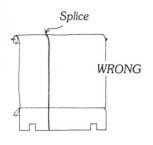

Splice

WRONG

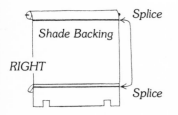

Splice

Shade Backing

RIGHT

Splice

Splicing

You may find that your backing or face fabric is not long enough or wide enough and you will have to make a splice. Think the problem through first. Chances are you can conceal the splice with some good planning.

Backing Splices

If you are making a shade with a fabric backing such as drapery lining, it may be necessary to splice it in order to make a shade wider than the standard 45-inch width of the fabric. For backings, always position the splice on the crosswise, not lengthwise, direction. This prevents any possibility of a streak running the full length of the translucent shade. Then think out the position of the splice even further. Plan it so it falls:

1. High on the shade where it will be rolled out of sight most of the time.

AND/OR

2. Low on the shade where it will be in or behind the slat pocket.

It is very important that the two edges of the fabric splice overlap very slightly, about $1/16$ to $1/8$ inch. This prevents a "dimple" or ridge on the right side of the shade and keeps a dark streak to a minimum. If a dimple does occur, it cannot be removed by pressing.

If you are splicing a commercial backing, overlap it by about $1/2$ inch and glue or bond the splice, depending upon the material. A splice in a blackout backing will not show through.

Face Fabric Splices

Should you find it necessary to splice a face fabric, the best choices for backings are a commercial backing (blackout if at all possible) or a fusible web method. Also decide whether you might be able to turn the fabric on the crosswise and position the splice high on the shade, or behind the slat pocket. Remember, too, that decorator sheets are wide enough not to require splicing.

When a face fabric is spliced, it is handled in the same manner as you would a bedspread or round tablecloth. The "seam" is not

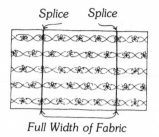

Splice   Splice

Full Width of Fabric

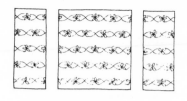

placed down the middle but is centered equally toward the *edges* of the shade.

To achieve a good splice cut the fabric edges with smooth clean strokes using very sharp scissors, making sure the patterns match. Draw a guideline for the center panel and press it into place first. Then proceed with side panels. Position the edges carefully on the backing, making sure they come evenly together before you press. Be careful to prevent stretching the edges as you work. Use an up/down motion of the iron.

For glued shades follow the general directions with the following adjustments. Draw a line for panel placement. Tape the center panel in place. Roll it back out of the way. Roll the side splices carefully onto short tubes. Roll the glue on the backing. Gently, roll out the center panel, aligning the cut edge to the guideline. Roll each side section into place carefully, matching the pattern as you go. Smooth it with your hands, iron, let dry, and continue with the shade.

STAGE 3: FINAL MEASURING AND CUTTING

The finished width of your shade is usually determined as follows:

Inside Brackets—shade cloth can often be as wide as, or slightly wider than, the barrel of the roller, as long as it does not rub and drag on the brackets.

Outside Brackets—usually ⅛ to ¼ inch from barrel ends to prevent rubbing.

Sash-Run Brackets—¼ to ½ inch from barrel ends to prevent rubbing on brackets or window molding.

Take care to be as accurate as possible. If a shade has not been accurately measured and trimmed to size, it may roll off center or not roll at all. To obtain best results use a carpenter's square or rafter-framing square for accurate 90° angles and straight edges.

1. Mark the long edges of the shade first, using two yardsticks taped together, a long metal ruler, aluminum bars, a venetian blind slat, or any long straight edge. Place the guide along one edge of the shade and line it up according to design or grain line. Using tailor's chalk or pencil, lightly mark the first long edge. Then reposition the guide along the other long edge. Take measurements at several points to be sure the two edges have been marked exactly parallel to one another.

2. Use a carpenter's square to mark the short ends. Then check once again that all angles are square and true and that sides are parallel. Carefully cut along the marked lines with sharp scissors, using long smooth strokes. Try not to lift or handle the fabric edges any more than necessary.

Carpenter's Square →   *Fabric*

3. While the fabric is still flat on the work surface, slide it over to the edge of the table so that it just barely extends over the edge. To prevent edges from raveling, run a little white craft glue along the edge. Put a little glue on your finger, then draw the glue along the edge of the fabric, just barely touching the edge of the fabric and leaving a small trail of glue behind. Pat the edge gently and wipe off any excess glue as you go. Treat top and sides, letting each dry before going on to the next.

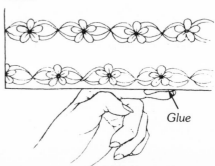

Glue

4. The slat pocket can be sewn or bonded. If your sewing machine will not handle the bulk or if your shade is very wide, it may be worthwhile to have a shade or upholstery shop stitch the pocket for you. Use long basting stitches to prevent cutting the fabric and be sure the tuck is straight. A crooked tuck makes the shade look crooked in the window.

- For a plain hem edge, turn a 1¼-inch hem to the back side of the shade. Machine stitch.
- For shades with decorative hems, sew the tuck higher on the shade. Turn the bottom up 10 inches. Stitch a 1¼-inch tuck so that it will lie on the front or back of the shade as desired.

Bonding the Slat Pocket
For Plain Hem Edge
Cut a 2-inch-wide strip of commercial backing. Using the paper liner as a press cloth, bond the strip so that it covers the fabric and makes a slat pocket.

For a Decorative Hem Edge
First draw two parallel lines. The first should be 7 to 8 inches up from the bottom of the shade, the second 2½ to 3 inches up from the first.

Then warm the backing with the iron. Join the lines and press the tuck. And remember to use a press cloth.

Finally, press a 1½-inch strip of backing evenly across the tuck.

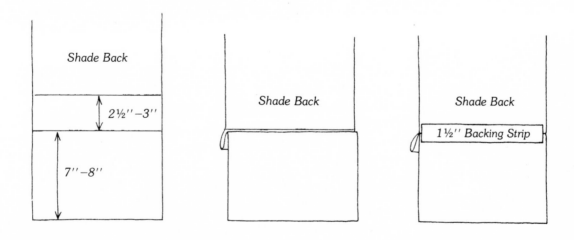

Shade Back

2½''–3''

7''–8''

Shade Back

Shade Back

1½'' Backing Strip

Purchased Trim

One or more rows of trim may be added to any shade style. Thick gimp or fringe should be glued with decorator craft glue or laminating adhesive.

Attaching the Shade

If your roller doesn't have a guideline on it, make one by holding the roller down firmly on a newspaper on a table or floor. Tuck your fingertips behind the roller so that it won't roll. Draw a line smoothly on the roller with a felt-tip pen or a piece of chalk. Using the guideline, center the shade and attach it to the roller with ¼-inch staples or tape. Be sure you have the roller and shade positioned correctly for the type of roll you want.

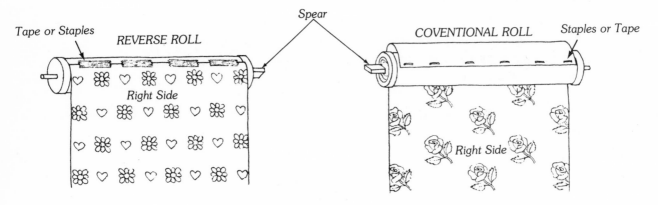

Equally as important as cutting the shade straight with all sides square is getting it attached straight and smooth on the roller. To test for a straight roll, pick the shade up off the table and roll it up gently. (If you try to roll it by pushing it along on the table you can often push it off center.) Then try it at the window in the brackets. If the shade rolls off center with one end apparently shorter than the other, reposition the shade on the guideline.

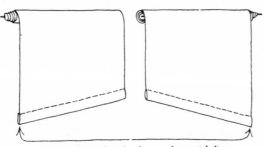

Reposition the shade on the guideline
Lift this end slightly   Retape to roller

Add a shade pull. This not only helps keep soiling to a minimum by keeping fingers off the shade, it encourages you to pull the shade in the center, the proper way to keep it on track and rolling straight.

NOTES ON CARE AND UPKEEP

• Shades that are used often won't collect dust. Dust them periodically with a soft brush or use a vacuum cleaner. If a shade needs spot cleaning, remove it from its brackets and sponge lightly with a damp cloth or use a spot lifter.
• Spraying the shade with a stain resistor will give it a head start on staying clean.
• For more complete cleaning remove the shade from the brackets. Unroll it on a flat surface. Wash it, piecemeal, with upholstery cleaner suds, taking care not to abrade the surface. Put it in the brackets and pull it down full length overnight or until it is thoroughly dry. Roll it to the top for twelve hours for a well-groomed, finished look.
• Nonwashable shades may be treated with a wallpaper refresher. An art gum eraser gives shades a quick cleaning, too.
• A too tight spring can be adjusted by rolling the shade up to the top, removing it from the brackets and unrolling it about 6 inches. Replace it in the brackets and roll it up again. Repeat until the tension is right.
• A too loose spring can be adjusted by pulling the shade down about 12 inches and removing from the brackets. Carefully roll about 6 inches onto the roller. Replace it in the brackets. Repeat until the operation is smooth.

Roman Shades

Roman shades are a popular window treatment and are similar to roller shades in that they pull up in a window, but they require more space at the top of the window because they pleat as they are drawn, rather than rolling out of sight. Roman shades require just enough fabric to fill the window area plus side, top and bottom allowance for hems.

While they do not require as much fabric as drapes, they take time to construct, to ensure that rings, cords and pulleys are accurately aligned.

Firmly woven fabrics make construction easier, although open-weave fabrics will work if they are handled with care. Print or plain fabrics may be used.

DETERMINING YARDAGE

When measuring for Roman shades, use a steel tape measure to ensure accuracy. Fabric may need to be seamed to create the necessary width. If so, seam one full panel in the center with two or more equal strips on the side. Be sure to allow for matching design where necessary.

Inside Mount
1. Measure opening height   ———
   Plus 4 inches for hem
       (more for deeper hem)   _4"_
   Plus 2 inches mounting
       ease   _2"_
   _____
   Total Length   ——— inches

2. Measure width of opening ———
   Plus 3 inches for side
       hems   _3"_
   _____
   Total Width   ——— inches

Outside Mount
1. Measure from top of window where the mounting board
       will be positioned to sill   ———
   Add 4 inches for hem   _4"_
   Plus 2 inches for mounting ease _2"_
   _____
   Total Length   ——— inches

2. Measure width from point to point where shade will overlap the window casing
Plus 3 inches for side hems   _____3″_____

Total Width   _____ inches

Lining

Most professionals feel shades hang better if lined. However, heavier fabrics or open-work casements may be left unlined. (Cut the lining to the width of the finished shade, minus 1 inch.)

CONSTRUCTION OF ROMAN SHADES— STANDARD METHOD

1. Pin the lining on the shade fabric, right sides together. (Shade fabric will be larger.)

2. Stitch ½-inch side seams. Pull inside out like a pillowcase, and press so that the lining is centered. Turn up a 4-inch hem. Press.

3. Turn the raw edge under ¼ inch. Stitch the hem. Stitch again 1 inch down to form pocket for weight bar.

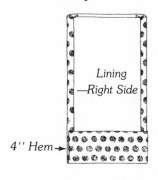
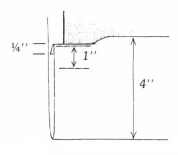

For a shaped hem, turn the fabric back on itself, right sides together. Stitch the hem shape, clip, turn, and press. (You may need to add extra length to shade for a deeply shaped hem.) Trim may be sewn or glued to hem if desired.

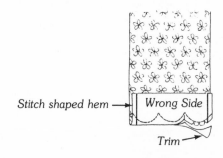

4. On the back side make marks for the rings. Keep the rings even and parallel. The first row is 1 inch in from the sides and at the top of the weight bar. Additional rows divide the area on the shade equally. Spaces should be no farther apart than 12 inches horizontally, and in fact it is better to space them at about 8 to 10 inches. This is important on looser weaves. Vertically, 5 to 6 inches is normal, but not farther than 8 inches apart. Rings can be sewn by hand or by using a button stitch on the sewing machine. (Sew through the fabric and the lining.)

When sewing by hand you may wish to change the thread color for the different colors in the fabric. When I do this, I thread several needles, each with the appropriate color. Then as I need to change color, I have the needle all ready to go. You may also purchase clear nylon thread for hand or machine sewing. Be sure it is not heat sensitive.

5. Insert weight bar (⅜″ metal rod) in pocket.

MOUNTING A ROMAN SHADE

1. Cut a 1 x 2-inch or a 1 x 3-inch board slightly narrower than the finished width of the shade.

2. Position screw eyes in mounting board directly above each row of rings on the underside of the board. You may need one extra eye to help distribute the strain of the pulling cords.

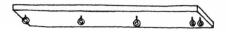

3. Staple the shade in place. If the shade is very wide, small pulleys or roller brackets (available through drapery supply) will help. They save wear and tear on the traverse cords.

Staples

Mounting Board

Shade Front

4. String the shade. Cut lengths of *non*-stretchy cord, one for each row of rings. Each will be a different length, but each one must go up the shade and across the top of the window with the excess at the side for pulling.

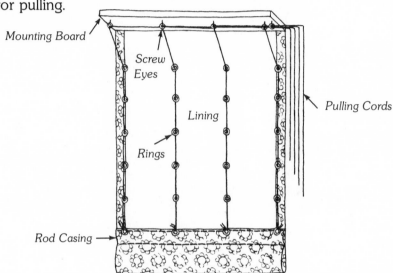

Mounting Board

Screw
Eyes

Lining

Pulling Cords

Rings

Rod Casing

5. Tie the cords securely to the bottom ring, and thread them through the rings and screw eyes. Final adjusting of the cords will be done when the shade is in the window. The screw eyes at the end where all of the cords come through must be large enough so that the cords don't bind.

6. Mount the shade in the window. For an inside mount, screw through board into the window frame or use angle irons. For an

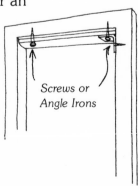

Screws or
Angle Irons

outside mount, use angle irons to mount the board above the window on the window frame or wall, as preferred. Adjust the cord tension so that each cord draws evenly. Knot the cords so that the tension won't slip.

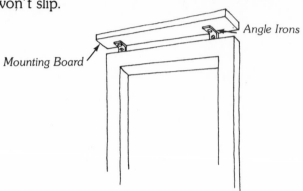

Mounting Board

Angle Irons

Mount an awning cleat at side of the window to wind off the cords when the shade is raised. To eliminate the awning cleat you can purchase tension cord pulleys (sometimes called *lock pulleys*) from drapery shops which work like those on venetian blinds. Pull the cords, then at an angle to the side to lock them in place. Pull to release them.

CONSTRUCTION OF ROMAN SHADES— RING TAPE METHOD

1. Follow steps one and two under standard construction method.
2. Turn up the hem and stitch it.
3. Stitch Roman shade tape vertically at the sides and about 10 inches apart on the body of the shade. Be sure the rings are level.

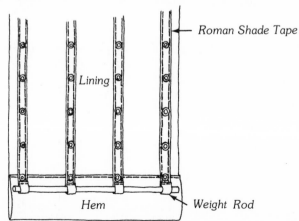

Roman Shade Tape

Lining

Hem

Weight Rod

4. Allow 2 inches of extra tape at the bottom to form loops for the weight bar.

5. Insert the weight bar through the loops.

6. Follow the steps on mounting described previously.

ROMAN SHADE VARIATIONS

A Counterbalanced Shade

A counterbalanced shade does not need awning cleats, but stays at a given level by lifting or pulling. The shade is constructed as described in the previous methods. However, two additional weights are needed, each equal to half the weight of the rod. B-B pellets or lead fishing weights will work very well as weights. Weights specifically meant for draperies are sold in dime stores.

1. String half of the cords in one direction and half in the other.

2. Attach the weights to the cords. Now the shade will stay at any point you raise or lower it to, because of the equally counterbalanced weights.

You can conceal the weight pouches with fabric, trim, or tassels.

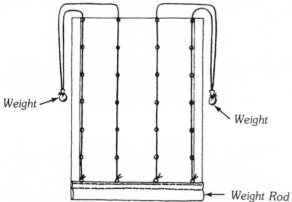

Weight

Weight

Weight Rod

Fishline Threading

Instead of rings and cords, fishline can be sewn through the shade at intervals, run through the screw eyes, and tied off and used to pull the shade. The line will make a nearly invisible lacing.

This is an especially good method for sheer fabrics.

Since fishline is usually nylon, it could become weakened by constant exposure to hot sunlight over a long period of time.

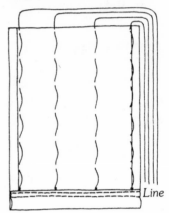

Line

Stitched Tape Tucks with Grommets

Grommets inserted in tucks stitched on the back of shades eliminate the need for rings, since the cords can be threaded through the grommets. Using twill tape helps support the weight of the fabric for large windows, or unusually heavy fabrics. Because the tape is stitched into the tuck only, there is no vertical stitching to show and clutter the front of the shade. Tucks this desirable, however. Determine the fabric length and add 1¼ inch for each horizontal row of rings.

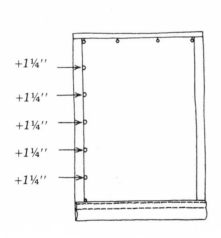

+1¼''

+1¼''

+1¼''

+1¼''

+1¼''

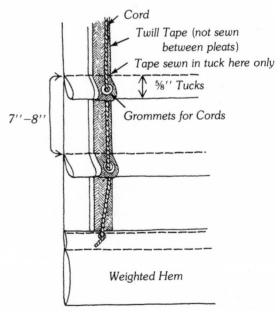

Cord

Twill Tape (not sewn between pleats)

Tape sewn in tuck here only

⅝'' *Tucks*

Grommets for Cords

7''–8''

Weighted Hem

Front and Back Stitched Tucks

Because of the narrow tucks stitching on the front and back of the shade, this method creates a very tailored shade that stacks neatly. Small tucks do not interfere with most designs. Dowels in front tucks are optional. They will help keep the shade crisp and straight if used. Eyelets in back tucks for cords eliminate the need for sewing on rings.

To determine the length add 1½ inches for each horizontal row of rings. (Remember there will be twice the number of tucks as in other methods.)

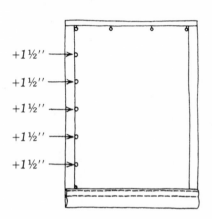

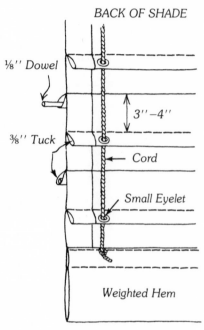

Hobbled Roman Shade

The hobbled Roman shade is like a standard plain Roman shade except that the pleats remain folded softly, even when the shade is down. This is an especially good method for plain colored fabric. The folds add interest and texture and hide the stitches that hold the rings in place. To determine the length of the fabric follow the directions for the standard Roman shade method and multiply by two.

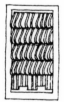

Follow the directions for a plain Roman shade, but before stringing the cords, mark strips of narrow twill tape (¼ inch) at intervals equal to half the distance between the rings. Tack the tape to the rings at the marked intervals, thus drawing up the pleats and forming a fold.

As an alternative you may mark positions for rings, then pin tape to the fabric at appropriate intervals, and stitch over the ring and through the tape and fabric, using the button stitch on your sewing machine.

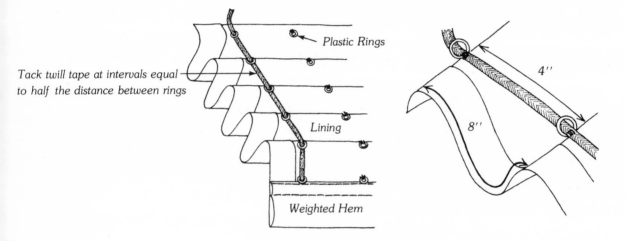

Tack twill tape at intervals equal to half the distance between rings

Plastic Rings

Lining

Weighted Hem

4″

8″

Austrian Shades

These softly draped and shirred shades make a formal and elegant statement at a window. They are most frequently made from sheer or silk-like fabrics, but may be made from lightweight prints as well.

DETERMINING YARDAGE

To determine amount of fabric needed, first measure the window width. Decide how many scallops you want and how wide they must be to cover the window. (Scallops should not be over 12 inches wide.) In order to maintain draping qualities of the fabric, an Austrian shade is usually not lined.

1. Width

    Measure the width of the window _____

    Multiply number of scallops times
       3 or 4 inches   _____

    Add 3 inches for side seams   _____

            Total Width   _____inches

Be sure to allow 1 inch extra for each seam if the fabric must be seamed to achieve necessary width.

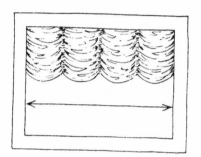

2. Length

    For sheers   Window length x 3 = _____ inches

    For opaques   Window length x 2 = _____ inches

CONSTRUCTION

Austrian Ring Tape Method

1. Sew the fabric panels together. Press 1½-inch hems on the sides and bottom. Stitch the bottom hem.

2. Cut lengths of tape, one more than the number of scallops. Be sure rings are aligned on the tapes. Tape is widely available in fabric stores and drapery departments.

3. Start 1½ inches down from the top and sew on tapes over the side hems and on the body of the shade, at evenly spaced intervals determined by number of scallops required for the shade. Be sure to keep the rings even. Knot the cords at the tape ends so

they can't pull out. Turn up the extra 1 inch at bottom and sew into the loops for the weight bar.

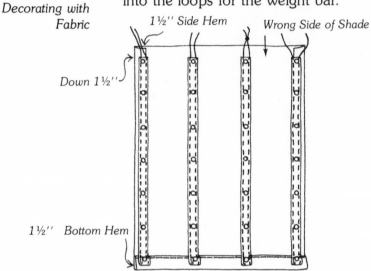

1½'' Side Hem

Wrong Side of Shade

Down 1½''

1½'' Bottom Hem

4. Since you have allowed up to 4 inches extra for each scallop, the shade will be much wider at the top than the window is. Pin tucks at the top on each side of the tapes as shown, until you have eliminated the extra width at the top.

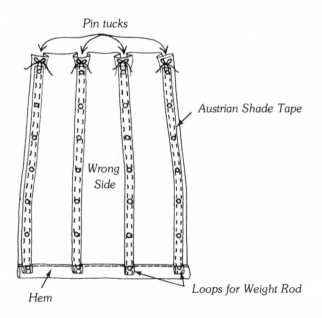

Pin tucks

Austrian Shade Tape

*Wrong
Side*

Hem

Loops for Weight Rod

5. A ⅜-inch metal rod will supply the weight for the shade. The weight is needed to help the shade operate smoothly. To help hold it securely in the loops at the bottom of the shade, first wrap the rod in fabric. You can glue it on, or cut a strip of shade fabric 2½ inches wide and 1 inch longer than the rod. Fold long edges ¼ inch to right side, insert the rod, turn in the ends, and hand sew the fabric in place. Slip the covered rod through the loops and tack it securely.

6. Pull the two knotted cords in each tape to gather the shade to the exact length of the window. Knot the cords to prevent gathers from slipping. Do not cut the cords.

When cleaning time comes, you can untie them and flatten the shade for easy handling. Make sure all the rings are still even across the shade after gathering.

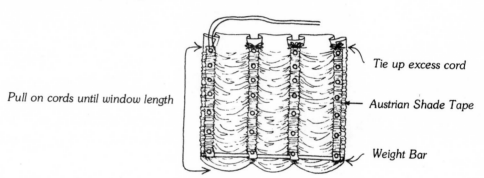

Pull on cords until window length

Tie up excess cord

Austrian Shade Tape

Weight Bar

7. To mount and string the shade, follow directions for a standard Roman shade.

Self-Tape Method

This is a particularly attractive method since the tapes are the same color and texture as the face fabric, usually creating much less bulk than shirring tape and a more uniform look on the outside of the house.

Follow the directions for ring tape method with the following exceptions.

1. Make your own tapes by cutting strips of self-fabric the length of the shade and 2 inches wide. Fold the edges to the center and press.

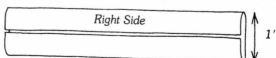

Right Side

1″

2. Lay the tapes in place on the shade 1½ inches down from the top. Thread the cords through the folds of the tape. Using an invisible (or regular) zipper foot, stitch the cords in place.

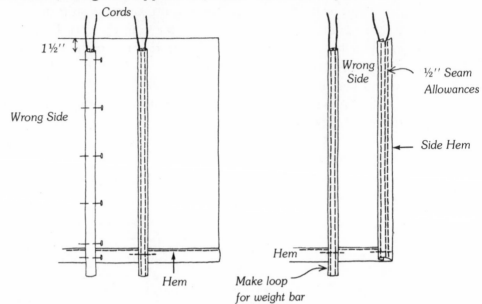

3. For hem edges fold and press a 1½-inch side hem and adjust the cords as follows:
- Stitch ½ inch from the edge of the shade.
- Insert two cords within the hem. Stitch the first cord next to the first line of stitching.
- Stitch the second cord next to the fold.

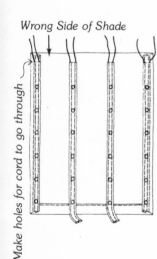

Sew the extra fabric on the center strips into loops to hold the weight bar. Sew small separate strips to the outside hems to hold the bar at those points.

4. Make small holes in the side hems to allow the cords through.

5. Sew rings to the tapes at intervals about 6 inches apart.

6. When all the cords and rings are in position, pull gently but firmly, drawing up the fabric to the desired finished length. Do not cut the cords. Tie them off securely in neat bundles.

7. Add the weight bar.

8. Mount and string as for standard Roman shade.

Additional Window Ideas

The following ideas, which require a minimum of fabric, create unusual effects. Adapt and alter them as you wish to fit your own needs.

KERCHIEF PANELS

Two flat panels of fabric sewn to fit the window, suspended from a dowel or café curtain rod and folded back, create a unique flat window treatment. Use two contrasting colors or prints for special effects.

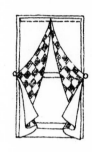

1. Make each panel half the width of the window plus 1 inch; and the height of the window plus 3 inches for hem and seam allowances.
2. Cut four pieces of fabric (two each from different colors), and stitch ½-inch seam allowances as shown, leaving 1½-inch openings at the top.
3. Fold under ½ inch and then 2 inches at the bottom for a hem. Sew the hem by hand.
4. Turn it inside out and press.
5. Sew a row of stitching 1½ inches down from the top to form a casing for the rod.
6. Sew a plastic curtain ring or fabric loop halfway down on the inside edges.
7. Hang the curtains in the window. Fold them back and attach a ring to a cup hook or ornamental hook or knob.

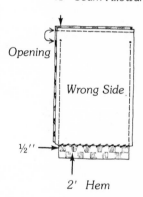

½'' Seam Allowance

Opening

Wrong Side

½''

2' Hem

This same technique can be adapted for floor-length window panels as well.

For a variation on the casing top, use flat ties cut from strips of fabric 18 x 4 inches. Fold the ties in half lengthwise and stitch the three open edges with a ½-inch seam allowance, leaving an opening for turning. Space the ties evenly across the top of the panel before stitching the lining and the panel together. Tie over a wooden pole curtain rod.

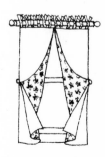

ROMAN PANELS

This is a variation of a Roman shade. It is moved manually, however, on a system of dowels. It is most appropriate for narrow windows, since the panels can become heavy and awkward with too much width. The advantage is that either the top or bottom part of the window may be uncovered by repositioning the fabric panel and crosswise dowels.

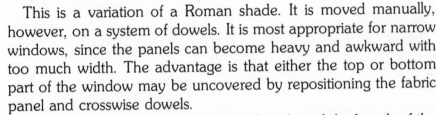

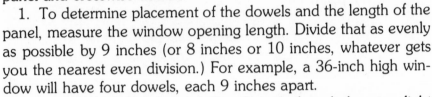

1. To determine placement of the dowels and the length of the panel, measure the window opening length. Divide that as evenly as possible by 9 inches (or 8 inches or 10 inches, whatever gets you the nearest even division.) For example, a 36-inch high window will have four dowels, each 9 inches apart.

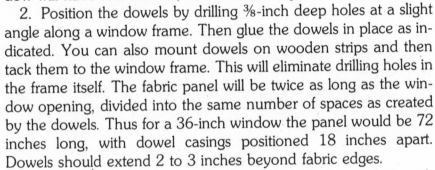

2. Position the dowels by drilling ⅜-inch deep holes at a slight angle along a window frame. Then glue the dowels in place as indicated. You can also mount dowels on wooden strips and then tack them to the window frame. This will eliminate drilling holes in the frame itself. The fabric panel will be twice as long as the window opening, divided into the same number of spaces as created by the dowels. Thus for a 36-inch window the panel would be 72 inches long, with dowel casings positioned 18 inches apart. Dowels should extend 2 to 3 inches beyond fabric edges.

9″
9″
9″
9″

36″

3. Prepare the panel as for the flat shade. (Use one fabric, with contrasting sewn-on strips for casings, if desired.) The panel can now be positioned at the window. To raise or lower the shade, reposition the cross dowels.

For an inside mount, this treatment may be adapted by cutting and installing wood "rests."

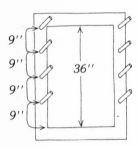

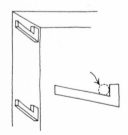

Cornices and Valances

Cornices and valances not only add a finishing touch at a window, but they also can conceal the hardware and mechanical workings of the window treatment as well. They are adaptable to any window style and treatment, from formal and traditional to light-hearted and contemporary. Since you can adjust the place-

The pictures on this page and the three that follow were taken in an old apartment building, where many walls were cracked or bulging. The fabric helped disguise these flaws, and it adds welcome color to the rooms.

The gathered valance and café curtains combined with gathered tiebacks make a bright window treatment in this heavily used kitchen, which looks out onto a dark city yard. The matching fabric walls make an attractive background for the open storage shelves.

See pages 32–67 for wall covering instructions and pages 74–94 for window treatments.

In this part of the kitchen, the wall fabric covers several imperfections. The "table", covered by a round, ruffled cloth, is actually a board resting on a small washing machine. Both the table and the fabric are easily removed and serve as camouflage for the appliance.

See pages 176–180 for table cloth instructions.

This "before" bathroom has not been redecorated for years. The purely functional shower curtain is mounted on a metal rod. The plaster walls are drab and peeling. An easy combination of fabric and time could make a big difference, as you'll see on the next page.

This bathroom, in the apartment directly below the one shown on the preceding page, looked just like it before redecorating. A new medicine cabinet and higher shower rod were put in, but the real change comes from the fabric. The bright pattern on the walls creates a bright new room. The high, gathered fabric shower curtain, on the same rod as the clear plastic inner one, brings it all together.

See pages 32–67 for wall covering instructions; see pages 198–200 for shower curtains.

ment of the cornice or valance on the wall or window frame, you can often use either of them to extend width or to tie together different sized windows for a uniform look.

Cornices are firm, architectural frames, usually made of wood. Frequently they are padded, covered with fabric, and then suspended over windows. Valances are made of soft or slightly stiffened fabric and are suspended in a similar manner. They are generally gathered, pleated, shirred, or swagged.

Of the many ways to construct a cornice or valance, one method may prove to be a bit easier for you because of the materials you have on hand, your past experience with tools, the construction of your home or apartment, or how permanent or temporary you want the cornice to be.

CORNICES

Stiffened Buckram

A very stiff woven and coated fabric called *buckram* is available through drapery (and sometimes millinery) suppliers. This fabric forms the base for a flexible yet sturdy cornice that can be mounted on a curtain rod or dowel.

1. Cut a buckram strip the length of the front of the curtain rod plus clearance. Add side returns if this is a box cornice.

2. Stitch a 2-inch strip of twill tape or drapery lining ½ inch from the top and side edges to form the casing for the rod.

3. Wrap padding, such as polyester fleece, around the buckram. Stitch it by machine, taking care not to stitch the rod pocket closed.

4. Cut the fabric 3 inches longer and 2 inches wider than the buckram. Lay the right side of the fabric on the wrong side of the buckram. Stitch a ½-inch seam.

Wrong Side of Fabric

Right Side of Fabric ⟶

5. Flip the fabric to the right side and finish the sides and bottom by hand.

Buckram may be cut into fancy or ornamental shapes and covered in the same manner. To trim the bottom edge, cut it with scissors, stitch it on a machine and glue the trim to cover the stitches.

Other stiffeners, such as nonwoven iron-on interfacings, commercial roller shade backings, or fabric bonded with fusible webbing can also be used to create stiffened cornices.

The only complaint I have ever heard about this method is that across very wide windows the cornice sometimes tends to dip inward or waver at the center. To avoid this problem, a mounting board or box-frame base is helpful.

Mounting Board Ideas

A board fastened above a window with angle irons, which are anchored to wall studs, can form the base for a variety of different cornice treatments. The board must be wide enough and long enough to clear the window treatment beneath by a couple of inches. You might also consider suspending the board from screw eyes mounted several inches in from the ends, which then hang on nails, picture hangers, or screw hooks mounted in the wall.

or 🔨 or

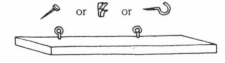

Then fold the top edge of the cornice over the board and staple in place.

- Or staple pieces of nylon fastening tape hooks to the board at intervals. Sew the fuzzy side to the cornice fabric in corresponding positions.
- Or preshrink snap tape, then staple half of it to the mounting board and sew half to the top of the cornice.
- Or preshrink hook and eye tape. Staple the hooks to the board, and sew the eyes to the top of the cornice.
- Or pad and fabric wrap a "frame" of Upson board®, foam board, or cardboard. Attach the frame to the mounting board.

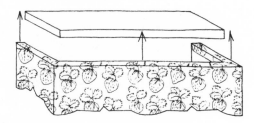

Another simple way to mount a padded cardboard cornice frame is to insert drapery hooks into the back of the cardboard and hang the frame over a curtain rod.

Drapery Hooks

Note that a mounting board cornice provides a built-in dust-cover for your window treatment.

Box Cornices

Traditionally, cornices are constructed of boards secured at the corners with angle irons, nails, or screws. Additional angle irons are used to attach the frame to the wall at the sides. When a boxlike cornice is constructed with a solid dustcover top, angle irons are usually attached to the top. For windows over 40 inches, add extra angle irons for more support. The cornice can just sit on the angle iron supports with small nails pounded through the holes keeping the board from sliding, but making it easy to remove for cleaning.

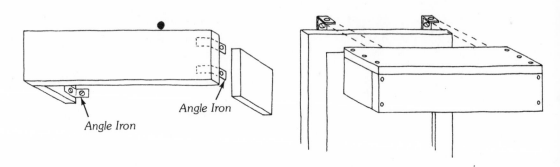

Angle Iron

Angle Iron

An easy cornice mounting consists of screw eyes, which are fastened to the window frame, and screw hooks, which are positioned on the cornice. Thus the cornice can be lifted on and off for cleaning, and the only marks on the wall are the holes from the screw eyes, which can be easily filled at a later date.

A similar method of mounting a cornice uses a combination of picture hangers and screw hooks. This is useful where the wall would not support a screw hook.

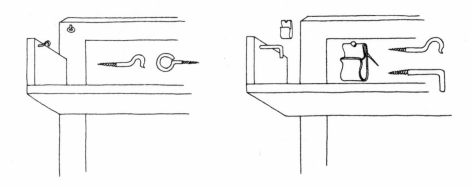

Here is a simple method for covering a cornice with fabric. Try cutting a pattern from brown paper first, if you are not familiar with cutting and wrapping techniques.

①

② Fold   Fold

Fold   Clip   Clip   Fold

Fold

③ Fold

Staple   Staple

④   ⑤

Wrap and Staple   Wrap and Staple

A Cardboard Cornice

Cut a sturdy piece of cardboard to size, then score it with a utility knife and bend it to form a lightweight cornice. Tape the sides together before covering it with fabric. Lightweight cornices of cardboard or foam board can be attached to walls with ordinary straight pins driven in with a hammer. If there is no edge to attach the cornice to, fasten a small block of wood to the wall first. Then glue the cornice or tack it to the block.

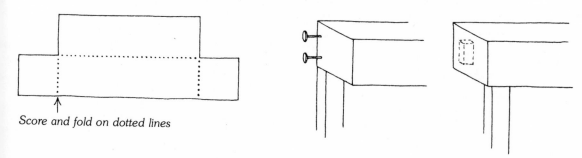

Score and fold on dotted lines

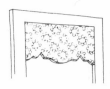

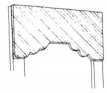

Flush Cornices

Here is a simple cornice that will fit flush inside a window frame to coordinate with a roller shade, venetian blinds, café curtains, or shutters. Wrap the board with padding and fabric, then attach it to the frame with angle irons. Flush mounted cornices may be mounted inside a window frame or doorway, or outside reaching edge to edge.

These cornices can be made from cardboard, Upson board®, or foamboard. They make lightweight, but sturdy cornices that can be "nailed" to the window frame with straight pins. Foamboard can be cut with a razor blade, utility knife, or even an electric slicing knife. Upson board®, like wood, must be sawed into shape.

VALANCES

Gathered Valances

1. Determine the length of the finished valance, adding 3½ inches for a top casing and at least 2 inches for a double bottom hem. For the width allow at least a double fullness plus the side hems.

2. Turn under ½ inch on the top edge then press a 3-inch hem. Stitch the bottom edge of the hem and stitch again 1 inch from the top folded edge to form a casing and a ruffle heading.

3. Make a double 1-inch hem on the bottom. Add fringe or trim if desired.

4. Thread the valance on a curtain rod. Adjust the gathers.

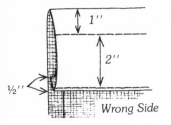

Shirred Valance

Shirring tape makes quick work of this valance. You can also make your own fabric strips, as shown in the section on Austrian shades. Choose between a shirred top heading or a completely shirred valance.

Four-cord shirring makes wide, attractive headings. Allow 1 inch each for top and bottom hems in addition to the finished length. Allow for at least double fullness. Hem the bottom, top, and sides. Stitch the shirring tape in place. Pull the cords (knotting ends to secure), until the valance is the proper length. Mount on a curtain rod with drapery hooks pinned into the back of the shirring or use a cornice-box frame or mounting board.

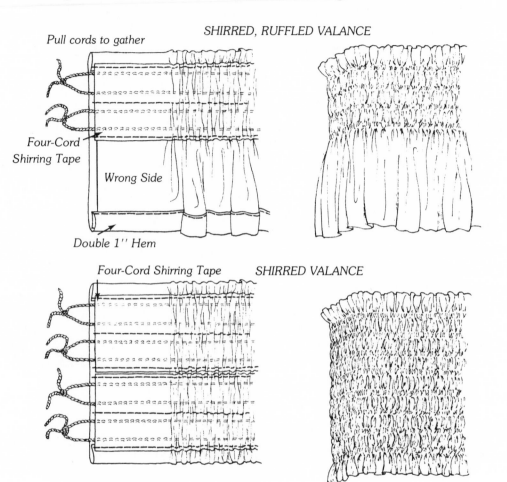

SHIRRED, RUFFLED VALANCE

Pull cords to gather

*Four-Cord
Shirring Tape*

Wrong Side

Double 1″ Hem

Four-Cord Shirring Tape *SHIRRED VALANCE*

Austrian Valance

For an Austrian valance allow for the width of the valance, plus 3 to 4 inches of extra fabric per swag, plus the side hems. For the length allow three times the finished depth plus 2 inches for the hem at the bottom. Hem the top, bottom, and sides. Stitch two-cord shirring tape at appropriate intervals. Tie the bottom ends of the cord so they won't pull out. Pull the cords to achieve the desired length. Knot the ends of the cords. Staple the valance to the mounting board, adjusting it to fit.

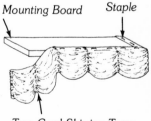

Mounting Board   *Staple*

Two-Cord Shirring Tape

Pleated Valance

A pleated valance is treated the same as a very short drapery (see p. 84). Use pleater tape or stitched pleats. Mount the valance on a curtain rod with drapery hooks or attach it to a mounting board. Pound U-shaped screen staples into the edge of the board at intervals that correspond to the spacing of the pleats on a valance. Be sure a pleat is positioned on the corners of the valance.

Corner Pleat

Staple

Drapery Hook

Swags and Jabots (Cascades)

Swags are elegant ways to treat your windows. They recall the classic and traditional effects from Europe and colonial America. They may be used alone for smaller windows or in pairs, three or more together. Jabots (or cascades) may be placed over or under the ends of a swag, in order to finish off the window around the return of the cornice board. Jabots look as though they are the ends of the swag, but they are in fact separate pieces. Swags hang better if lined. Jabots are nearly always lined because both sides show when they are pleated.

For accuracy, always make a muslin pattern for both swags and jabots. It will drape softly, as the finished treatment must do. For mounting it is best to make a cornice box frame with a ¼-inch plywood front. Although a mounting board can be used, the swag and jabots may tend to cup under after they have been hanging for some time.

1. Once the cornice is prepared, determine the depth of swag (average depth about 15 inches) by pinning a tape measure to the cornice and letting it drape (A-A). Decide how wide you wish the pleated area to be (B-B), usually about 5 inches from each end of the cornice.

2. Mark the muslin according to your measurements.

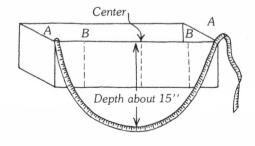

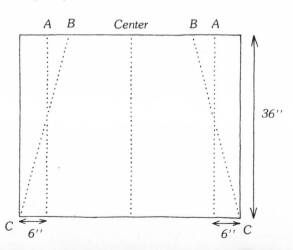

3. For five folds in a swag, divide the lines you've drawn from B to C into 6 equal parts and mark them clearly on each side. For 6 folds divide into sevenths, for seven folds divide into eighths.

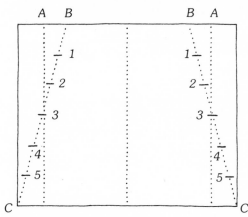

4. Pin the muslin into place across the top of the cornice. Fold the muslin on the first marks and tack it to the cornice at B, folding and shaping the fabric and matching the center line. Continue to form each fold in succession.

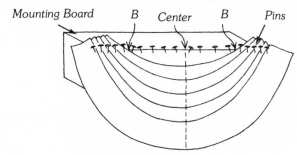

5. When you are satisfied with the drape of the swag, trim off excess fabric at the top and along the curved bottom edge about 4 inches below the last fold.

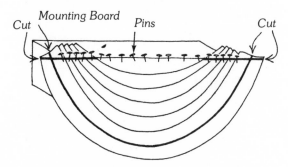

6. Remove the pinned pleats from the cornice and smooth them flat. You will have a notched piece that is your pattern. Place the right sides of your fabric and lining together. Pin the pattern to them. Cut out the swag pattern pieces. Then sew the bottom curved seam. Clip, turn, and press. Re-align the notches.

7. Re-pleat the swag. Bind the top edge with twill tape. Mount on the cornice.

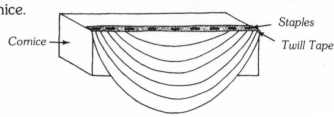

Jabots (Cascades)

1. To make the muslin pattern, measure the jabot to return around the end of the cornice with a total width of about 25 to 35 inches. The long edge will be about 27 to 30 inches long. The short side is usually the depth of the swag (about 15 inches).

2. Lay the fabric and the lining right sides together and cut according to pattern. Stitch ½-inch seam allowances, leaving the top open. Clip, turn right side out, and press. Staystitch the top edges.

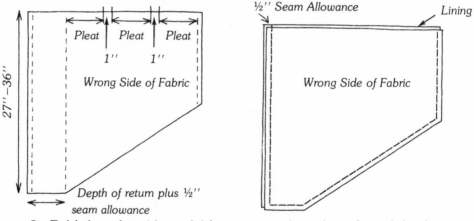

3. Fold the jabot (three folds is average) so the edge of the first fold is along the edge of the return. Allow about 1 inch between the pleats with a total of about 6 inches across the front. Press the pleats. Duplicate in reverse for the other side.

4. Bind the top edges and mount them under or over the swag.

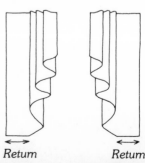

A Simple Draped Swag/Jabot

1. Mount a pair of post-type drapery holdbacks at or just above the corners of the window frame. Measure between posts for A-A. Drape a tape measure over the posts to determine B-B and B-C.

2. Cut the fabric and the lining, right sides together.

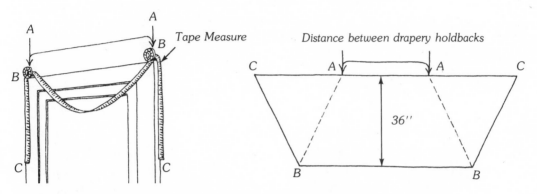

3. Stitch around the swag, leaving an opening for turning. Clip, turn, and press. Close the opening.

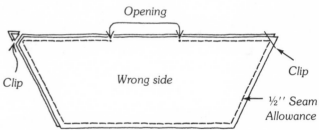

4. Stitch two-cord shirring tape or self-fabric tape and cords across the back of swag from A to B.

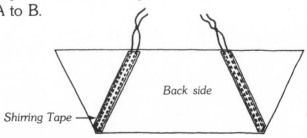

5. Pull up the cords, gathering the swag. Adjust the swag and jabots over the post holdbacks. For wider windows staple it to a mounting board for more support.

Decorative Hems for Roller Shades, Cornices, Roman Shades

As you consider decorative hem ideas for your window treatments, look around you for guidelines. Think about things like:
- Architectural features in the room—arches, moldings
- Furnishings in the room—period and style, texture, lines
- The design on the treatment fabric—scallops, notches, curves, straight edges

Try to create a hem treatment that will be in harmony with the room and its decor.

After you have thought of what hem treatment you would like, make a paper pattern. For scallops and curves use plates, saucers, platters, curved sewing rulers, or other rounded objects. Fold a piece of paper in half and work out the design. Make the strip 6 to 10 inches deep and the width of the shade or cornice. Try several ideas until you are satisfied with one. Cut out the design and open out the paper. Place the pattern on the hem edge and weight it or clip it in place so it won't move as you trace the design. Be sure the design is even. Cut it out with sharp scissors (for roller shades), or hem the edge or wrap it around the shaped cornice, depending on the project. You might add one or more rows of fringe, bias, gimp, or cording as a decorative touch.

FOUR

FURNISHINGS AND ACCESSORIES: DETAILS WITH A DIFFERENCE

Fabric-covered furniture—pieces other than those we normally expect to be upholstered—can spell excitement and economy in decorating. You can cover unfinished or second-hand store finds and give them an expensive, custom look. Accessories are the important details that really fill in and complete the overall picture in decorating. Your fabric-covered accessories not only add the finishing touch of coordination, they are also a great way to use up fabric pieces and scraps left over from larger projects.

One idea will lead to another. Use the following ideas as a springboard to start your own imagination working.

Chair and Bench Seats

Chair and bench seats are easy to cover and can add unusual fabric interest to a room. Usually you need to remove only four screws from the chair underside to gain access to the seat.

A layer of polyester fleece under the fabric yields several benefits. It opaques, often making it unnecessary to remove the old covering before applying a new one; it pads softly; and it gives the fabric a surface to cling to so that it lies smoothly without drag lines. If you want to cover over good fabric somewhat temporarily, you can add a layer of thin plastic like a plastic bag. This prevents spills from penetrating to the good fabric. It is also a good idea to spray the finished seat with a fabric protector, too.

141

1. Measure the depth and width of the chair seat. Add 3 inches all around. Cut fabric and fleece to these dimensions.

2. Staple the polyester fleece to the seat first. Clip to fit as needed and remove any excess bulk from the corners.

3. Wrap and staple the fabric in place; wrap the ends first, working from the center outward. Then staple the sides in the same way. Pull the fabric snug and smooth it at the corners using lots of staples if necessary. Don't cut the excess from the corners unless it is necessary due to a heavy or bulky fabric.

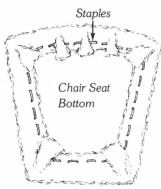
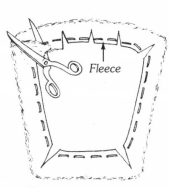
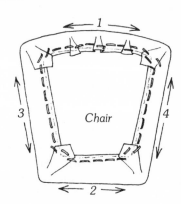

UPHOLSTERED CHAIR SEATS

For chairs that have nonremovable seats with backs or arms in the way of the fabric, slashes must be made to accommodate the covering.

1. Determine the size of the fabric piece by measuring from the bottom of the seat at the center back up and over to the bottom of the seat at center front plus 4 inches (A). Measure from the bottom of the seat at the side front up and over to the opposite side plus 4 inches (B). It is sometimes easiest to remove the old cover carefully and use it as a pattern.

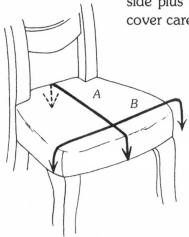

2. Center the design on the seat with the fabric wrong side up and pin it in place to the seat. Fit it to the front of the seat by pinning darts at the corners.

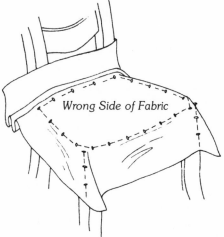

Wrong Side of Fabric

3. Lightly mark the outline of the top edge of the seat with tailor's chalk. Remove the fabric from the chair and stitch the front pinned corners. Trim the seam allowances to ½ inch, turn the fabric right side out, and replace it on the chair to check for a smooth fit. Mark a cutting line from the center of each back leg to the edge of the fabric. (If desired, reinforce the area behind the slashes with a strip of iron-on interfacing.)

Line for cutting

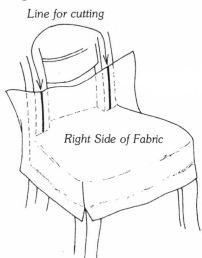

Right Side of Fabric

Push gently

Right Side of Fabric

Clip and tuck under

*Clip and
tuck under*

4. Cut carefully only part way down each line. Pull the fabric between the legs at the back of the chair, clipping a little more along the cutting line as necessary to get the fabric to lie smooth when the raw edges are pushed down between the seat and the legs. The remaining fabric then may be wrapped and stapled to the underside of the chair. Also, cording may be applied around the bottom edge by removing the cover and stitching the cording around the bottom on the right side of the fabric. Clip the seam allowances of the cording so it goes around the back corners. Trim away any excess fabric at the back corners.

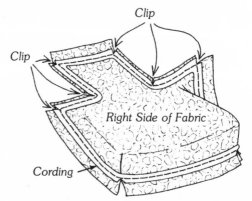

Clip

Clip

Right Side of Fabric

Cording

5. Place the cover on the seat and turn the raw edges of the seam allowance and the cording to the wrong side around the back legs so that the cording turns up. Clip it to the stitching line of the cording at the front legs. Tuck the seam allowance under at the legs, then pull the fabric under the frame at the front, back, and sides and staple or tack it in place. Finish the bottom of chair by covering it with dark fabric or muslin, folding the edges under, and stapling or tacking it in place.

Muslin

Staples

For other chair ideas see "Tie-Ons" in chapter 7, "Quick and Portable."

Stretcher Bar Art

Any fabric can become a work of art when it is stretched firmly on a frame for hanging, but vividly colored, imported fabrics are especially effective mounted this way. Use softwood art stretcher bars available in art supply stores, needlework departments, or fabric stores. They are available in precut, premitered lengths in two-inch intervals ranging from 6 to 72 inches. All you need are four strips to create a desired frame size. The staple gun is easiest to use for this project, but you may use a hammer and tacks instead.

1. Select a fabric and determine its placement and the part of the design you want displayed. Choose art stretcher bars accordingly. Cut the fabric at least 2 inches wider and longer on each side for ease of wrapping.

2. Push the stretcher bars together to create the frame. Use either a carpenter's square or two adjacent edges of a table to be sure the frame is square.

3. Center the frame on the wrong side of the fabric. Use push pins in a few places to hold it while you check it from the front side to be sure everything is centered properly. Then bring the fabric over the bars and staple it at center top and center bottom, keeping the fabric taut.

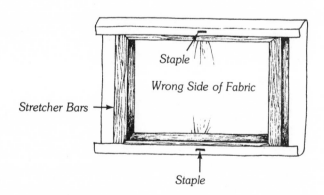

4. Repeat at the sides, pulling snugly to eliminate slack in the fabric.

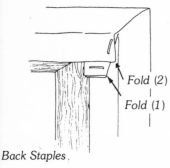

Fold (2)

Fold (1)

Back Staples

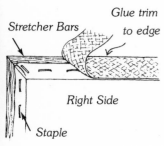

Stretcher Bars

Glue trim
to edge

Right Side

Staple

5. Start at the center of each strip and staple toward the corners, stopping about 1½ inches from the end. Be sure to do the top and bottom first, then the sides.

6. Finishing the corners smoothly is a two-step process. Smooth the fabric along the stretcher bar. Pull it snugly into a mitered fold and staple it in place. Pick up the remaining fabric and smooth it into a sharp corner, wrap it to the back, and staple it in place on the top of the first fold.

7. Your work of art is ready to hang. If the fabric is not quite tight enough, spray it with a little water or hold a steam iron above the fabric and let the steam penetrate to shrink it slightly.

Some fabric designs do not allow enough space around them for a two-inch border for wrapping without cutting into an adjacent design. If this is the case you may wish to staple the fabric to the edges of the frame and then glue decorative woven or knit trim to hide the raw edges of the fabric.

If you have pulled too tight in one or two places, causing a bulge in a design line, remove those staples and the fabric will spring back in line. It is easier to correct this on the finished panel rather than as you go along.

Fabric can also be wrapped around a solid piece of wood, cardboard, foam board, fiberboard, and so on. Depending on the substance you choose, several different techniques may be used. Consider staples, spray adhesive, starch, and fusing. Try unusual groupings of stretched art as well as single large panels.

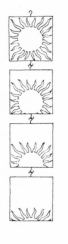

Wall Hangings on Rods

Fabric as well as tapestries, rugs, bedspreads, and needlepoint may be mounted and displayed on rods or dowels. If the fabric is lightweight, it should be backed to give it body and prevent stretching. An iron-on interfacing or fusible web and plain fabric can do the job.

1. Choose the fabric, allowing enough extra length at the top and bottom to sew a casing for the size of the rods or dowels you have chosen. If your fabric is a bordered type with no length for casings or hems, create them from bands of a solid complimentary-color fabric stitched all the way around the fabric edges. Hand or machine hem the sides, then sew the casings at the top and bottom for the rods.

2. Insert the rods or dowels. Add a cord for hanging or decorative tassels if desired or appropriate.

Other ideas:
- Try fabric art in chrome or gold gallery frames for an elegant touch.
- Plastic boxlike gallery frames also show fabric to unique advantage.

Folding Screens

Don't overlook the versatile folding screen in adding an exciting dimension to your decorating skills. The techniques are similar to those for covering chair seats and stretcher bars, and the small amount of construction necessary is simple for anyone to do. I've been making folding screens for years with no special tools other than a hand saw, carpenter's square, hammer, and utility knife.

If you've never used folding screens, start by becoming aware of them in furniture store displays, model homes, and model rooms, and decorator magazines. You'll see them used to:

- Introduce color
- Add lines and angles
- Create a focal point
- Create a room divider between a dining/kitchen or sewing/bedroom
- Reverse to introduce new color or pattern
- Hide storage space
- Conceal pipes or architectural features
- Conceal a TV set
- Create a background for plants

Hint: The same techniques you use to cover screens can apply to shelves, shutters, wall panels, tables, wall hangings, and doors.

BASIC CONSTRUCTION AND WRAPPING TECHNIQUES

If you are making a short or a two-panel screen, solid ¾-inch plywood or solid boards may be used. You might also consider using damaged bi-fold closet doors, louvered or plain. But when your screen will be four or more panels, open construction is a better technique because the screen will be lighter weight and easier for you to manage. You may use stretcher bars for your framework. The most common construction is done with 1 x 2 inch wood strips from a lumber yard.

Building the Framework

1. Cut 1 x 2 inch lumber into desired lengths. Include the crosspieces for the top and bottom and at least one interior brace. Join the sections by pounding in Skotch® wood joiners (which are best when used on both sides of the frame), or corrugated fasteners. Use a carpenter's square to make sure the framework is square.

2. Glue or tack thin cardboard, Upson board®, or poster board to each side of the frame. This gives you a hollow-core door that is lightweight and opaque to light.

3. Then wrap the panels in fabric and hinge them together using regular hinges or bi-fold folding screen hinges. The latter are a little more expensive, but they flex in both directions, giving

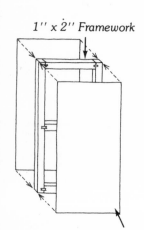

1″ x 2″ Framework

Upson board®, Cardboard, or Posterboard

more versatility to the screen. For a custom effect that softens the look and feel of the screen, pad the panels with polyester fleece or quilt batting before wrapping them with fabric.

Wrapping Techniques

Two-Piece Technique, Method 1

Wrap and staple or tack the fabric to the back side of the panel using the same techniques as for stretcher bars. If the screen is to be against a wall, no further treatment is needed. If you plan for the screen to be seen from both sides, cover the back by gluing, fusing, or tacking on a fabric cut to fit.

Two-Piece Technique, Method 2

Wrap the fabric around the panel from each side and staple the edges. Then apply a decorative trim, fusing or gluing to hide tacks or staples.

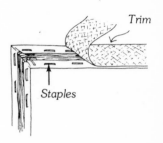

One-Piece Technique (Also can be used for shelves)

1. Cut the fabric 4 inches longer than the panel and wide enough to wrap completely around the panel plus 2 inches. (Be sure to center or match design for each panel before cutting fabric.)

2. Wrap and clip at each corner, then wrap and staple.

3. To finish the final edge, use glue, fusible webbing, or a cardboard upholsterer's strip (upholsterer's tape) and brads.

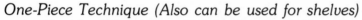

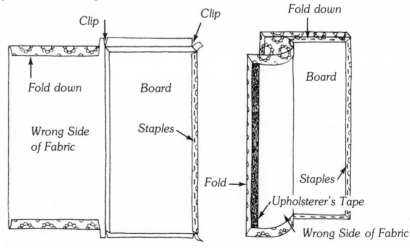

Slipcovered Technique

Sew a fabric slipcover for framework panels or pieces of cardboard or Upson board®.

1. Measure the circumference around one panel. Multiply this by the number of panels you have. Allow ½ inch between panels for cardboard, 1 inch for a wood frame. Make a small test sample to determine how much space between panels is desirable with your fabric to allow the screens to fold easily.

2. Stitch each panel-width closed. Leave the amount of space between each that you have decided on. Remember that you need to leave a little more space in the slipcover for each panel to allow for the thickness of the panel.

3. Slip panels into place and close the opening by stapling or hand stitching.

Hint: If wood frame folding screens are to rest on hardwood floors, chair glides pounded into the bottom of the frame will help keep the fabric clean.

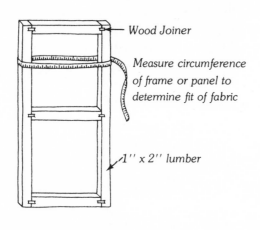

Wood Joiner

Measure circumference of frame or panel to determine fit of fabric

1″ x 2″ lumber

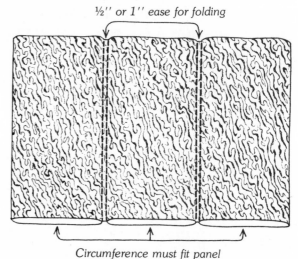

½″ or 1″ ease for folding

Circumference must fit panel

Cardboard Screens

Inexpensive cardboard three-panel folding screens are available in some furniture stores and notions departments. Although they are preprinted with a design, you can cover them with a design of your choice, by wrapping them in fabric by spray gluing or fusing.

An even more economical screen, and one that is completely flexible, can be created by taking a large and sturdy cardboard shipping crate that once held a refrigerator, freezer, sofa, or mattress, and cutting it into panels.

1. Cut the panels to the desired size. Lay them down flat, side by side. Leave about ½ inch between each one. Cover them with fusible webbing. Place the fabric on top of the webbing, centering the design. Make sure you have cut enough webbing and fabric to wrap completely around the panels. Iron the fabric to the first panel. Check the spacing between panels and be sure they are even at the top and bottom. Iron succeeding panels.

2. Turn the panels back side up on your work surface, smoothing the fabric and webbing. Wrap the top edge over the end of the panels and fuse it in place. Wrap the side edges over the panels. Fuse. Fold the bottom edge up so it is even with the top edge of the screen when the entire fabric piece is folded into place.

3. Fold the fabric up and into place on the panels and fuse it down. Add narrow strips of webbing under the final edges of fabric and fuse them in place. If you prefer, you can wrap all four edges of the screen, then fuse a separate piece of fabric into place on the back side.

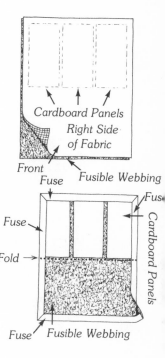

Shelves

INDIVIDUAL SHELVES

Wrapping shelves with fabric before placing them in brackets gives them a new dimension. To wrap a board or shelf follow the same directions as for covering a folding screen panel.

Another quick, easy way to wrap fabric around shelves is to use liquid starch. Cut the fabric 4 inches longer than the shelf and wide enough to wrap completely around it plus 2 inches for overlapping. Then, using a sponge, apply starch liberally to one side of the shelf. Apply the fabric and smooth it in place. Adjust and position stripes or other design. Then liberally sponge starch on the outside of the fabric, too. Continue around the board, clipping fabric to fit and sponging on more starch under and on top of the fabric. Allow it to dry. You may need a bit of glue or fusible web to secure the last fold. The starch will keep the fabric taut.

FABRIC STRAP SHELVES

To make five shelves, fasten two 1 x 3 inch boards 6′ 4″ long vertically to a wall. Screw 6 heavy-duty cup hooks or screw hooks to boards 18 inches apart, leaving 1 inch at the top and 3 inches at the bottom. Cut 10 straps 8 x 32 inches, from sturdy canvaslike fabric. Fold in half lengthwise. Stitch as illustrated, with ½-inch seam allowances. Turn, press, and topstitch. Add ¾-inch grommets on each end of the straps. Hang the straps on hooks. Insert 1 x 10-inch shelves into the straps.

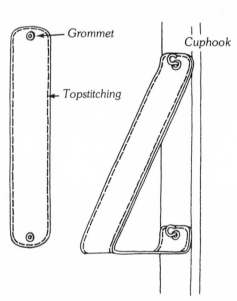

QUICK SHELF-TABLE

Mount a fabric-covered board on decorative brackets beside your bed, or mount it as a narrow shelf in an entry or hallway.

Bookcases

To cover a bookcase with fabric:

1. Cut two pieces of fabric twice the depth of the shelves plus 3 inches. Clip along each shelf edge as illustrated.
2. Wrap the fabric to the inside and secure it.
3. Cut a piece of fabric for each shelf to be covered—the length of the shelf plus 2 inches for turning under, the circumference of the shelf plus 2 inches for overlap.
4. Secure the shelf strips to the bookcase.

Consider covering other items such as file cabinets, recipe boxes, trunks, chairs, and so on.

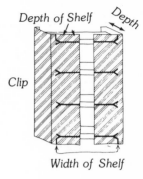

Depth of Shelf · Depth

Clip

Width of Shelf

Chest of Drawers

If your chest has an unusual shape or style it will be best to think through your plan of attack, even making a paper pattern first to help you visualize how and in what order the fabric should be applied. Gluing or starching will be the best methods as a rule. Stapling may be satisfactory on basic square shapes. Basic instructions for covering a chest of drawers follow.

1. Clip and wrap fabric around the sides of the dresser first, allowing an overlap of 1 inch onto the dust frame, and wrapping fabric to inside of the dresser.
2. Cut fabric strips to wrap dust frames. Secure in place.
3. Cut and trim a piece of fabric for the dresser top. Fold or miter the corners to fit. Wrap the drawer fronts in the same way.

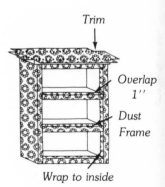

Trim

Overlap 1''

Dust Frame

Wrap to inside

Trim or fold corners

Parsons Tables

The classic lines of the Parsons table are particularly suited to fabric decorating. It takes very little fabric, and the table can be recovered from time to time as your mood or decor changes.

TWO-PIECE METHOD

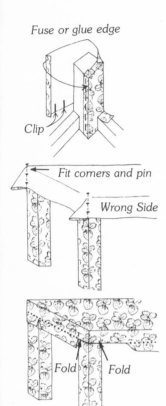

Fuse or glue edge

Clip

Fit corners and pin

Wrong Side

Fold   Fold

1. Cut the fabric for covering the top of table 10 inches longer and wider than the table top. Cut four strips for the legs to go around each leg plus 3 inches, and length of the leg plus 3 inches. Starting at the inside corner, wrap the leg, clipping the fabric as needed where the leg meets the apron of table. Fuse or glue the final edge in place or turn the hem back over upholsterer's tape and tack it with brads.

2. Place the top fabric on the table wrong side up and pin darts at each corner so the top fits over the table like a slipcover. Stitch the darts, then cut away excess fabric, leaving ¼-inch seam allowance. Turn it right side out.

3. Clip the top piece where the apron meets the table leg. Tuck the fabric under, pull the remaining fabric under the table, and staple or fuse it in place. *OR*

Position the top fabric piece right side up on the table. In turn fold each corner under, creating a 45° angle. Wrap the fabric under the table and fasten it in place. Add a chair glide to each leg.

ONE-PIECE METHOD

Many Parsons tables can be covered by a one-piece method. If your fabric has a directional design, however, this method is not satisfactory, as it results in the pattern being upside down on two legs.

1. Cut the fabric the length of the table and its legs plus 6 inches.

2. Center the fabric on the table. Glue, fuse, or temporarily tack it in place to hold it while you work on the legs. Fold the fabric into 45° miters at the corners and press to mark the crease lines. Draw lightly to transfer the line to the bottom layer with tailor's chalk.

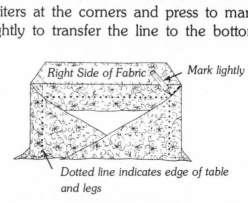

Right Side of Fabric   Mark lightly

Dotted line indicates edge of table
and legs

3. Cut along the legs as indicated by the dotted lines in the diagram, and fold this top piece back out of the way on the table top.

4. Smooth the fabric around the ends of the table. Cut as indicated by the dotted lines, then wrap any excess around the leg to the inside.

5. Treat the other ends of the table in the same manner. Finish off the final edges of legs as described in the two-piece method. Wrap the flap from the top down and under the table to finish it.

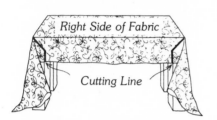
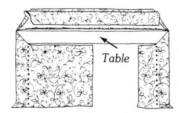
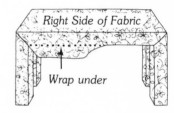

Fabric-Covered Cubes

Cubes are a simple solution to the end table/coffee table problem. If they are hollow with hinged or liftoff tops, they become extra storage too. Fabric can be stapled, glued, fused, starched, or slip-covered in place.

Fabric-Covered Picture Mats

Fabric-covered picture mats are colorful, add texture and interest, and are easier to make than traditional bevel-edge, knife-cut mats. Because mat board is only available in a limited range of colors, you will find the endless color range available in fabrics to be an added advantage.

1. Measure the picture you wish to frame. Cut a mat the same size or larger, if you wish, from thin cardboard or poster board. Cut the fabric 2 inches wider and 2 inches longer on each side for

Dotted lines indicate cutting lines

2″

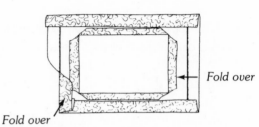

Back of Mat

Fold over

Fold over

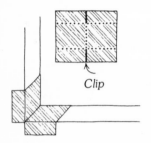

Clip

handling ease. (If fabric is bulky, trim it to fit the mat instead of wrapping it to the back.)

2. Use spray adhesive or fusible web to attach the fabric to the front of the mat. Clip and trim away the fabric in the center.

3. Fuse or glue the fabric to the back as illustrated.

Note: If you use thicker material for the mat (or picture frame or mirror frame) first cover each corner with a small piece of matching fabric and then proceed with the wrapping as just described. Corrugated cardboard, for example, will require this treatment. If the frame is much thicker than ¼ inch it may be preferable to use the four-strip method described for picture frames.

Picture Frames and Mirror Frames

Fabric-covered frames can create unexpected interest in room accessories. One of the simplest methods requires four strips of fabric, each cut about 2 inches longer than the frame (longer if frame is very thick), and wide enough to wrap around the frame.

1. Apply the fabric to two opposite sides first, clipping it to fit as you go. Glue, starch, or fusibles can be used.

2. Fold the two end pieces to create mitered corners. Apply them to the frame. If you prefer, you may overlap fabric at corners and double-cut through with a razor blade, peeling away the overlapping areas. The bias will not ravel.

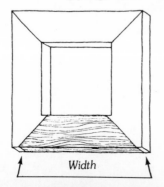

Width

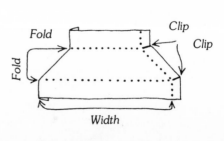

Fold

Fold

Clip

Clip

Width

Oval or round frames require lots of clipping and trimming on both the inner and outer edge to allow fabric to be pulled flat and taut to the back side. Allow plenty of fabric if you plan to pad the frame.

● Any frame takes on a special look when one or more layers of quilt batting are applied under the fabric. This quilted and padded look can be very effective on mirror frames in particular. If you quilt or pad your frame, stapling is the easiest technique to use.

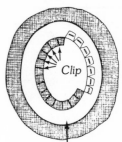

Back of Frame

Cardboard and Other Storage Boxes

Desk accessories, recipe boxes, gift boxes, and even the larger filing and coffee table-size boxes available in notion departments are all candidates for fabric covering. They are easy to cover and wear well, to provide color, texture, and enjoyment for a long time.

1. Measure the box, determining each dimension to figure the amount of fabric needed. Position fusible webbing on the top of the lid, then cover it with the fabric. Iron the fabric to the top of the lid.

2. Place the lid upside down and trim away the excess at corners as shown in the diagram.

3. Fuse the sides numbered 2 to the lid, bringing the fabric just around the corner onto side 3. Fold the sides numbered 3 into place and fuse them to the lid. Add more webbing or a little glue to the fold at the corner.

4. Wrap the remaining fabric to the inside of lid and fuse.

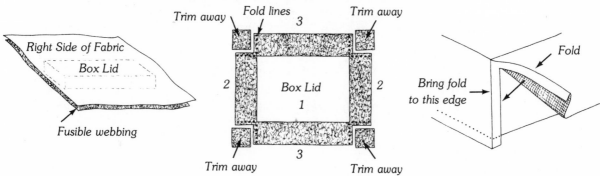

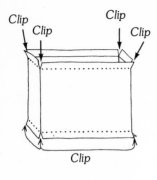

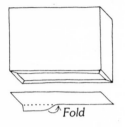

5. Treat the bottom of the box in the same way unless you are working with a directional fabric where the design must be upright. In that case, use the circle method illustrated in the diagram. Wrap the fabric around the box, clipping and fusing it to the inside and to the bottom.

6. Apply a separate piece to cover the bottom, if you wish.

The best appearance and most durability is usually achieved by using solid webbing under a fabric, rather than using strips, but you may feel that strips will do the job satisfactorily.

Lining Trunks and Drawers

If you're hooked on antiques but find the rough interiors of the old pieces are hazardous to the things you want to store, or if you simply want to try something a bit different, try fabric linings. Patchwork decorating is a perfect way to line items of this kind, since individual patches are easy to apply and often fit the mood of the furniture.

Patchwork Decorating

If you love the casual look and early American effect of patchwork, you'll be happy to discover that patchwork is one of the easiest ways to decorate. It has the added advantage of being a terrific way to use up scraps and pieces of fabric.

Nearly any of the projects in this chapter can be patchworked in an instant. The methods you can use include craft glue, fusible web (a great way to use up webbing scraps, too), liquid starch, and spray glue.

Gather as many scraps of fabric as you think you will need.

Remember that there is some overlap. Just lay on one scrap at a time in a random pattern, clipping at corners as needed and wrapping into place. You needn't limit yourself to small projects. I had a student who once starched a patchworked wall in her daughter's room in this way—using starch; it couldn't be easier.

If warping or raising a musty smell is a problem, fusible webbing is the answer, since it is a dry method.

If you prefer to line your older items with a single design and larger pieces of fabric, the following directions will make it easy.

1. Cut a strip or strips of fabric the depth of the drawer plus 2 inches. Try to use a selvage or folded edge around the top to prevent raveling.

2. Use the circular method and apply the fabric inside to the drawer sides, clipping at the bottom corners and applying the extra 2 inches onto the drawer bottom.

3. Cut a separate piece of fabric to fit the bottom and attach it.

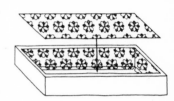

Lampshades

Can you cover a lampshade? Of course you can—it's easier than you think. Almost any fabric can be used, from silk to burlap.

Here are some guidelines to remember.

• Darker fabrics allow less light to pass through the shade.

• A design on the old shade will still show through a light-colored fabric when the light bulb is turned on.

• Burlap creates a nice texture, but tends to fade in bright sunlight. (But—faded burlap can be painted to restore a bright look.)

• Center the main part of the design at the center front on a flared shade.

FLARED

There are two methods for making a pattern for a flared shade. Depending on the size and shape of the shade, one may work better than the other. Regardless of the method you use, always make a paper pattern first.

Method 1: Rolling the Shade

Place the shade on the paper. Mark the beginning point on the shade and roll the shade along, carefully marking the top and bottom of the shade as you go. Add 1 inch for overlap. Cut out the pattern and test the fit on the lampshade.

1″ for Overlap

Method 2: Wrapping the Shade

Tape tissue paper snugly around the shade, overlapping the ends. Trace the outline of the shade and the seam through the paper. Add 1 inch for overlap. Cut out the pattern and test the fit on the lampshade.

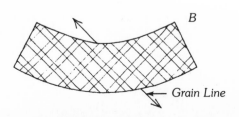

Mark Center Overlap

Preparing the Fabric

If your fabric has a directional pattern, cut the fabric as indicated in illustration A in order to keep the design centered and upright. If your fabric is geometric in checks, polka dots, or all over design, it will look better at the back seam if it is cut on the bias as in illustration B.

Fabric may be cut to fit to the edges of the shade with trim glued on to cover any raw edges or cut with a ¾-inch allowance for turning to the inside of the shade. Glue the fabric in place inside the shade, then glue on a trim to cover the raw edges. A decorator craft glue is best here, because it is fast drying and flexible.

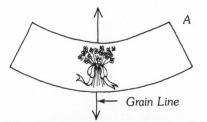

A

Grain Line

B

Grain Line

On this page and the three that follow you'll see table fabrics and other decorative accessories you can make.

Here, a floor-length round cloth with short, contrasting table topper above it adds a gracious note to a dining area.

See pages 176–182 for table covering ideas and instructions.

Above: Floor-length round cloth with matching runner and placemats. See pages 176–182 for instructions. Below: Floor-length round cloth with contrasting square table-topper and napkins to match bottom cloth. See pages 176–182 for instructions.

Above: Folding screen, lampshade, umbrella stand made of sono tube, storage cube, and reverse harem pillow. See pages 147–151, 159–167, 212–213, 208, 169–170 respectively for instructions. Below: Floor-length round cloth, placemats and napkins, and wrap and staple chair seat. See pages 176–182 for table fabrics and pages 141–144 for chair seat.

Before and after chairs: The chair above had seen better days. The chair below was recovered using the wrap-and-staple technique. Note that the seat covering has been stapled on, and braid or other trim needs to be applied to cover the staples.

See pages 141–144 for instructions.

Attaching the Fabric

One of the following methods may be used to attach fabric to a lampshade:

White Glue   Using a decorator craft glue, spread the glue thinly and evenly. Place the shade on the fabric and smooth the fabric in place with your hands.

Spray Adhesive   Spray the fabric evenly with the adhesive. Press the fabric onto the shade. This works best on smooth surface shades.

Starch   Spread the starch on shade using a sponge. Smooth the fabric into place. Let it dry. Add starch to the top is necessary. The starch method works only on smooth surfaces.

Fusible Web   Cut the fabric and a matching piece of fusible web. Place a web on the shade with the fabric on top. Using short strokes, work your way around the shade. Remember—no irons on plastic shades.

PLEATED

Pleated lampshades look much more complicated than they are. They take time and some patience, but you can create your own custom shade if you are willing to try. To help determine the depth of the pleats, look at commercial shades of similar size and style. Larger or very flared shades may require 1 to 1 ½ inches deep. I find, however, that I use ¾-inch pleats as a general rule. Smaller pleats are harder to make accurately and control. I once tried a shade with ½-inch pleats—never again.

1. Determine the yardage needed.
   Height
   For firm fabrics
   Height of shade plus ½ inch = _____ inches

   For fabrics that ravel
   Height of shade plus 1 inch = _____ inches

Length
Top circumference of shade $\times$ 2 = _____ number of pleats

Number of Pleats $\times$ 1½ inches
  + 12 inches = _____ inches

For straight drum shades or slightly flared shades use this easy formula: 3 x top circumference + 12 inches = _____ inches length of fabric strip.

2. Medium-weight fabrics are easiest to work with. To make light fabrics (gingham or sheets for example) firmer, dip in starch solution, then hang to dry. Press.

3. If the fabric needs to be pieced, do not seam it. Instead lap one piece on top of the other and fuse it. Keep the fabric pieces straight.

4. Prepare a strip of nonwaxed shelf or butcher paper, cutting it to the height of the shade plus ½ inch and the length determined in step 1. All edges should be perpendicular and parallel. Lay the paper down, cover it first with webbing and then with the fabric. Press until thoroughly bonded. With heavier fabrics it may be necessary to press on the paper side as well.

5. Trim firm fabrics with sharp scissors next to edge of paper, just barely cutting the paper to obtain a clean sharp edge. *Or* Turn ravelly fabric over the edge of the paper and fuse or glue.

6. Taking care to keep the lines straight and parallel, draw lines ¾ inch apart (or the depth of pleat you have selected) on the paper side. Use a see-through plastic ruler for ease and accuracy of marking. Every eight or ten pleats, use a carpenter's square or T-square to check that the lines are straight.

7. Hold the ruler at the line and lightly score with a blunt object such as a knitting needle or the edge of a spoon. Be careful not to cut through.

8. Fold the accordion pleats. Run the flat side of a knife or iron over bundles of five or six pleats to sharpen the edges.

9. Attach the pleating to the shade or hoops by one of these methods:

• With a tape measure for your guide, punch a hole every ½ inch just under the wire rim. (Use a large needle for punching.) Thread the needle with clear or matching thread. Anchor the thread and go through the first hole from inside to outside. Barely catch the fold of the pleat. Go back through the same hole and on to the next. Continue around the shade, pulling each pleat up snug as you go. Bobby pin the pleats in place around the bottom of the shade. Adjust the spacing. Put a drop of glue under each pleat. Let it dry. Remove the pins.

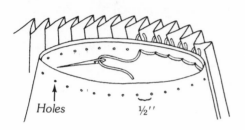

Holes   ½''

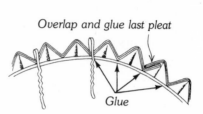

Overlap and glue last pleat

Glue

• Both the top and bottom of the shade may be bobby pinned and glued. Divide the top of the shade equally and make your marks for gluing the pleats. Glue and pin them. Adjust the bottom as just described.

• If you are attaching pleats to a wire frame, punch small holes ¼ inch down from the top edge. With fine yard or thread loop around the top wire. Repeat this for the bottom of the shade.

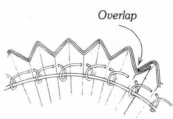

Overlap

10. To finish the shade, the last pleat should overlap in and not out. Trim off any extra pleats. Put glue along last pleat. Clip and let it dry. Remove the clips. If a small raveling occurs along the top or bottom edge, touch it with a little craft glue or trim with sharp scissors.

COVERING A COMMERCIAL PLEATED SHADE

If you already own a pleated shade of plastic or light-colored fabric, you can cover it by gluing (or starching on plastic). Cut the fabric as described in the preceding section, but allow 2 inches extra height. Then brush glue on three or four pleats. Push and fit the fabric carefully into the pleats, using a butter knife or flat plastic ruler for smoothing. Leave it until it is nearly dry. Clip if necessary with bobby pins. Then continue working, a few pleats at a time, on around the shade. Doing just a few pleats at a time prevents the damp fabric from pulling up out of the pleat and bridging the crease. When the fabric is dry trim excess fabric at the top and bottom with sharp scissors and touch with glue to control any ravels.

FITTED BELL SHADE

This type of shade must be cut on the bias to ensure stretch and fit. It is also fabric lined, so four pieces of fabric must be cut. Opaque, silklike fabrics work best.

1. Wrap the ribs and hoops tightly with narrow strips of twill tape or hem tape. This is not absolutely necessary, but it does give a more professional, finished product.
2. Pin the fabric to the shade, wrong side out and on the bias to establish seam lines. The fabric should be pinned so that the seams fall on the top of the ribs. Use clothespins to hold the fabric in place at the top and bottom and to prevent marring the fabric. Trim away any excess fabric, leaving 1 inch extra at the top and bottom. Remove fabric. Stitch the seams. Trim.

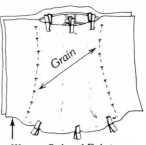

Wrong Side of Fabric

3. Adjust the outside shade fabric in place, again using clothespins to hold the fabric to the hoops. Tack the seam allowances to the ribs if necessary. Fold the top and bottom edges over the hoops and whipstitch them into place.

4. Position the lining on the inside of the shade. Fit it in place as just described and whipstitch the lining to the outside edge of the shade. Make small cuts at the braces to allow the lining to fit smoothly. Cut and fold a strip of shade fabric and wrap it around the top braces, hiding the small cuts in the lining fabric. Tack it in place at the top outside edges as shown. Trim the ends.

5. Attach trim to cover any raw edges at the top and bottom. Use bias-folded strips of the shade fabric or other trims of your choice.

It is possible (though not necessarily easier) to cut this shade with one seam by rolling the shade for a pattern and cutting the fabric on the bias. The fabric is then stretched very taut to complete the shaping and to locate the seam.

SHIRRED AND RUFFLED SHADE COVER

This is a quick, versatile shade cover. It has a soft look and can be accented with eyelets, lace, ribbons, and trim if desired.

1. Measure the height of shade and add 5 inches. Measure the bottom circumference; multiply it by two for fullness and add a 1-inch seam allowance.

2. Seam the ends with a ½-inch seam allowance to form a cylinder. Turn under the top edge ½ inch, then 1¾ inches, and hem. Turn the bottom under ½ inch, then ¾ inch, and hem.

3. Stitch shirring tape to the back of the top just below the hem. Pull the cords so the fabric gathers up to fit the shade snugly. Secure the cords.

4. Add ribbon or trim accents if desired. You may wish to starch the shade to give it a little more body. Try it on the lamp first.

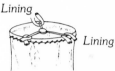

Lining

Lining

Right Side

Lining stitched in place

SHIRRED AND RUFFLED SHADE/COVER

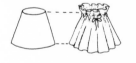

Hem

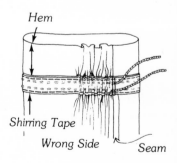

Shirring Tape

Wrong Side

Seam

GATHERED SHADE COVERS

A shade cover creates a very attractive soft shade. It consists of a gathered casing, which can be slipped over the existing shade. The advantage of a shade cover is that it can be removed, washed, and replaced. It can conceal a soiled or faded shade and is a good way to introduce texture and a feeling somewhat like a pleated shade with much less time and fabric invested.

Tiffany Shades

1. Cut the fabric equal to the height of the shade plus four inches and the circumference plus 4 inches.

2. Seam the short ends together. Then fold raw edges under ⅛ inch. Turn the folded edge under ⅝ inch and stitch to form a casing. Leave an opening for a drawstring or elastic.

3. Adjust the fabric on the shade with a drawstring or elastic. With tailor's chalk mark the bottom edge of the shade frame. Remove and flatten the fabric. Add fringe, trim, eyelet, lace, and so on. Replace it on the frame.

Follow the same directions for a very flared shade, except you may wish to add a little more fullness in the bottom circumference.

Drum Shades

1. Cut a strip of fabric equal to the height of the shade plus 4 inches and the circumference × 2. The strip may be seamed if necessary. Seams can be hidden in the gathers.

2. Seam the short ends together. Then fold raw edges under ⅛ inch. Turn the folded edge under ⅝ inch and stitch to form a casing. Leave an opening to insert a drawstring or elastic.

3. Cut a ⅜-inch elastic and run it through the casings, drawing it up so that the cover fits the shade snugly. Remove any excess elastic, sew the ends together, and close the openings by sewing.

Ruffled Top and Bottom

Victorian Fringed

Turned-Under Casing

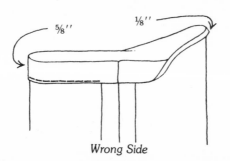

⅝″ ⅛″

Wrong Side

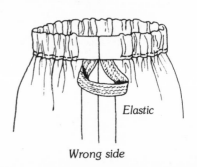

Elastic

Wrong side

This same technique can also be used to make attractive wastebasket covers and flowerpot and planter covers.

FLUTED SHADES

The directions for fluted shades are based on a full circle. To determine if your lampshade is a true fluted circle, look at it from underneath. If there is no seam, it is a circle pattern. Sometimes the base of the shade is fluted and the crown is a flat cone. To create a pattern for the cone, it may be easiest to cut a strip of true bias (see chapter 1) and stretch and fit it to the shade top.

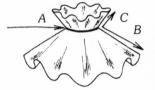

1. Measure the circumference of the throat (narrowest part) of the shade (A). Measure the depth of the shade (B) and the depth of the crown (C).
2. On paper draw two circles with the same circumference as C. To do this, first determine the diameter of the circle as follows: the circumference divided by 3.14 equals the diameter. Draw a line equal to the diameter. Find the middle of the line and use a compass to make the circle.
3. From the outer edge of the circle just draw and measure out the distance of the depth of the shade (B) at several points. Connect the lines to form a circle.
4. Repeat step 3, but measure the distance of the depth of the crown (C) to make a smaller circle.
5. Cut out each circle. Make a slash through from one side to create an opening.
6. Fit each circle on the shade to check for fit. Then cut them out from good fabric and glue them to the shade with spray glue or craft glue. Add trim, bias tape, or ribbon at the throat and at the top and bottom to conceal raw edges.

When you fit the pattern to the shade if you find the edges of the pattern do not quite meet because of the thickness of the fabric, cut two half circles with ½-inch seam allowances instead of the full circles as indicated in steps 3 and 4. This adjustment will allow enough extra fabric to allow for bulk.

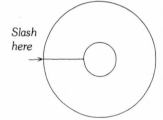

*Slash
here*

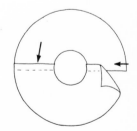

Overlap seam allowance

Wastebaskets

Wastebaskets are always fun to fabric as accessory items. Treat flared baskets the same as flared lampshades.

• Measure and cut a straight strip of fabric for drum or cylinder shapes. Add fringe, trims, ribbons, lace, or other ornaments.

• Use the same directions as for gathered lampshade covers to create an attractive shirred cover which you can slip right off for laundering.

• Paint the basket, then starch, glue, or fuse on decals cut from fabric scraps. Or create a patchwork effect using many scraps.

Pillow Potpourri

Probably no other single accessory can do as much for a room as a grouping of pillows. The possibilities range from a collection of accent pillows to floor seating, to a sofa built of pillows. By mixing and combining sizes, shapes, colors, and textures, you can create your own mood and excitement. Whether you prefer bright colors or a mixture of textured neutrals, you can't go wrong with pillows,

Look through magazines and stores for pillow ideas. Any basic pillow style can be changed by cutting the basic pattern into strips or sections to be seamed together in different colors or fabrics. It is wise to make a paper pattern for changes or new pillow designs.

KNIFE-EDGE PILLOWS

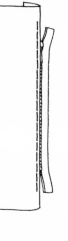

These pillows are among the simplest to make and are the basis for the four styles that follow. Knife-edge pillows are thicker in the middle and taper to the edges. The opening through which the liner or filling is inserted may be closed by stitching or by zipper.

Square or Rectangular Shape

1. Cut two squares or rectangles of fabric the desired pillow size plus a ½-inch seam allowance on all sides. Press under the

seam allowances on the two sides where the zipper will be inserted. Center the zipper and stitch along the folded edge of one section as shown in the diagram.

2. Overlap the second piece so the stitches are covered. Tape them in place. Use the edges of the tape as a guide and stitch the zipper ends and the side.

3. Fold the fabric back so the right sides are together. Sew from the zipper around the other three sides and back to the zipper. To keep lighter-weight fabrics sharp in the corners you may want to fuse a triangle of iron-on interfacing to each corner before stitching the pillow.

4. Turn the fabric right side out. Press. Insert pillow liner or stuffing.

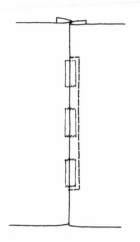

Round

A round knife-edge pillow with a zipper is usually constructed as illustrated.

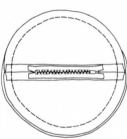

HAREM PILLOWS

These are my favorite pillows. And fortunately they are simple to make.

1. Cut two squares or rectangles of fabric the length of the pillow you want to cover plus half the depth desired on each side. Make a knife-edge pillow as described previously.

Length of Pillow

Half of Depth

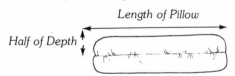

2. Mark each corner on an angle. For most pillows about 2 to 3 inches in from the corner is adequate. Gather the fabric evenly between your fingers and tie it securely with a string. Do not trim the corners. Be sure the zipper you install is short enough so that it will not be tied into the corners.

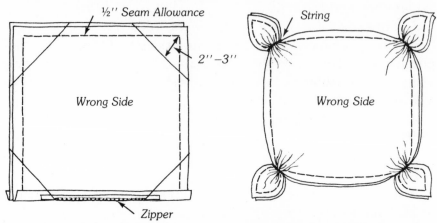

3. Sew a liner from a sheet or muslin, making it an inch or two larger than the outer case. Do not tie the corners of the liner. Stuff the liner with shredded foam or polyester fiber fill. Close the liner. Insert the liner in a harem cover.

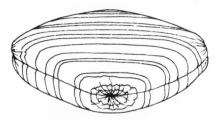

FINISHED HAREM PILLOW

BOX PILLOWS

Box pillows have a top and bottom piece with a plain or shirred fabric side piece. They are even in height from the center to the sides.

1. Cut two pieces the length and width of the finished pillow plus ½-inch seam allowances on each side. Cut three strips for the side panels. One strip should be long enough to go around

three sides of the pillow. The other two should be equal to one side in length and half as wide as the depth of the pillow plus seam allowances.

2. After inserting the zipper, sew the side pieces together. Press the seams. Pin the pillow bottom to the side pieces, clipping and spreading and boxing corners as needed. Stitch across the corners to blunt and strengthen them.

3. Repeat with the top pillow section. Turn, press, and insert foam block or stuffing. The only difference in a round box pillow is that an inset is required for the zipper placket and a great deal of clipping will be required to allow the fabric pieces to lie flat and smooth.

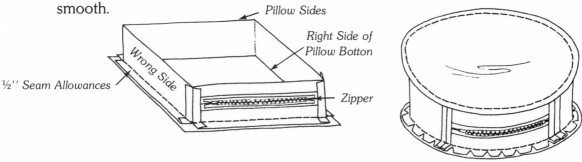

Pillow Sides

Right Side of Pillow Botton

Wrong Side

½″ Seam Allowances

Zipper

ROUND BOX PILLOW

Cording

You can add cording to any of these pillows by stitching the cording just inside the seamline before final stitching.

MITERED BOX PILLOWS

Unlike the classic box pillow, the mitered box style has a box shape but no separate inset box strip. Hence it is easier and faster to sew.

1. Cut two squares or rectangles of fabric the desired length and width plus half the desired pillow depth on each side. (See step 1 under "Harem Pillow.") Add ½-inch seam allowances. Make the pillow following the directions for knife-edge pillows.

2. Center two adjacent side seams one over the other and stitch a line to form a triangle. The length of this line determines the depth of the pillow.

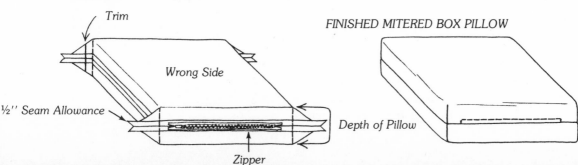

Trim

FINISHED MITERED BOX PILLOW

Wrong Side

½″ Seam Allowance

Zipper

Depth of Pillow

TURKISH PILLOWS

This style is similar to the mitered box pillow, except that the corners have a softer look created by the folded tuck corner detail.

1. Measure and cut two fabric pieces, following directions for harem pillows.

2. Fold and mark each corner of the two pillow pieces in the following manner. Fold the corner in half, wrong sides together. Measure half of the depth of the pillow and mark it with chalk or tailor tack. Clip the seam allowance to mark it.

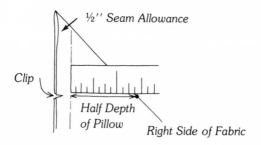

3. Open the corner. Then fold each side into the middle, bringing the clips together. Baste the folds in place.

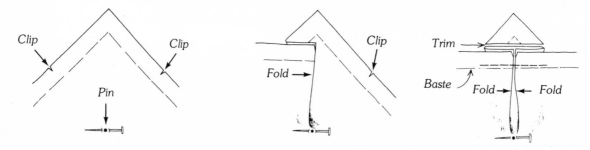

4. Place the right sides together and machine baste one seam allowance. Insert the zipper. Open the zipper. Stitch the remaining seams and match the corners exactly keeping the folds straight and even. Insert the liner.

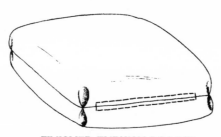

FINISHED TURKISH PILLOW

SELF-BORDERED PILLOWS

The border area may be flat or slightly padded. Pad it by including a layer of fleece or quilt batting cut the same size as the fabric pieces. Then stuff the center area to desired plumpness.

1. Cut two squares or rectangles of fabric to the finished size of the pillow plus ½-inch seam allowance on each side. Place the right sides together. (Add padding as mentioned above if desired.) Stitch around the edges with ½-inch seam allowances, leaving an opening for turning.

2. Turn the fabric right side out. Press. Topstitch 2 to 2½ inches from the edge. Stuff inner area, paying particular attention to filling corners.

3. Machine stitch the inner opening closed, then topstitch the entire outer edges of the pillow.

If you want a zipper closing, place it in the center back in the same manner as for a round knife-edge pillow.

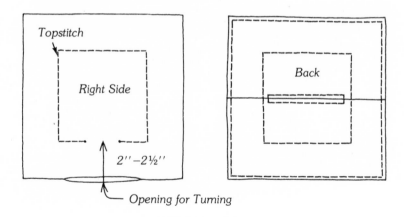

ROLLING PIN PILLOW

This is an unusual style that can be made in many sizes. It's great for a neck roll, a TV-watching pillow, or just because you like it.

1. For a base use a round piece of bolster foam wrapped in two or three layers of quilt batting (A), or a firm roll of quilt batting (B).

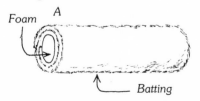

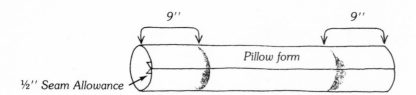

9'' 9''

Pillow form

½'' Seam Allowance

2. Wrap the base with fabric, allowing 9 inches of fabric on each end (or 3 times the finished length of the knob on the end of the pillow). Slipstitch or sew the seam by machine after pinning it to fit and locating the seam. Then slip the cover over the form.

Any time you are trying to slide a close fitted cover over foam or batting which tends to be sticky, wrap a plastic bag (like those from a dry cleaner) around the object first. Then pull the cover in place. It will slide much more easily. The plastic can be left in place or torn or pulled out.

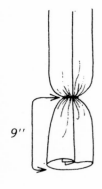

9''

3. Tie the ends of the roll snugly with several wraps of string. Square knot securely. Flatten out the ends of the fabric so they are overlapped with only right sides showing.

4. Fold the fabric ends back a third of the length, then fold once more.

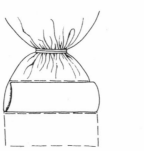

5. Wrap the fabric around itself, first one side then the other, tucking the ends in. Tack the knob to the pillow and tack the overlap.

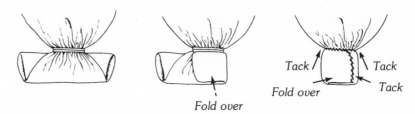

Fold over

Tack   Tack

Fold over   Tack

6. The finished pillow will have two sturdy knobs or handles on the ends.

ROLLING PIN PILLOW

Variations

For variations make a sleeve casing, but trim the ends by turning them back on themselves or adding eyelets or ruffles. Fold one half of the ends back inside and stitch them in place with a casing for a drawstring. Or add ruffles. Use bias tape or self-fabric for a casing if the fabric is not turned back inside. You may also eliminate the casings, and just wrap and tie the pillow ends with ribbon or trim.

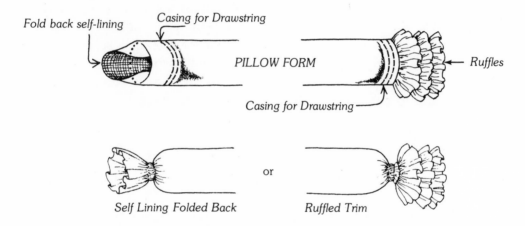

Fold back self-lining   *Casing for Drawstring*

PILLOW FORM

Ruffles

Casing for Drawstring

Self Lining Folded Back   or   *Ruffled Trim*

For another variation, make casings that draw up just to cover the pillow ends. Then stitch trims to extend beyond the ends when the drawstrings are tightened.

Casing for Drawstring

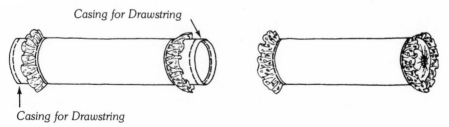

Casing for Drawstring

FIVE

FABRICS FOR THE TABLE

Beautiful and unusual table linens set a festive dining mood. It's easy to customize table linens to suit your needs, and they're especially easy to make to suit your decorating scheme. Large cloths, of course, require planning for design placement and yardage requirements. Napkins, mats, and runners are quick, excellent ways to use up scraps and odd pieces of fabric.

Table Cloths

Many fabrics make excellent table linens. You'll want to consider vinyls, soil-release, and permanent press fabrics because of their easy care. Sheer lace over solids and lightweight or heavier weight fabrics will all serve you well. But avoid heavily textured fabrics, felt, satin, or velvets that require special cleaning and will not wear well. Also beware of uneven plaids or stripes, diagonals, and obviously one-way designs.

Consider using quilted fabric or a machine- or hand-quilted fabric of your own design. Old quilts may also be used. Quilted cloths, especially on round tables, have a beautiful drape and hang and add an unexpected note of softness. They also eliminate the need for padding or a silencer underneath.

Hint: Make your own silencer by using a layer of polyester fleece under any cloth. It reduces the noise of china and silver against the table and at the same time adds a smooth layer of protection for your tabletop.

Don't overlook the advantages of sheets used as table linens. Their size, beautiful designs, and permanent press qualities make them naturals for this purpose. You can make a 100-inch cloth in minutes, with no seams to worry about. This handy guide to sheet sizes will help you select the right sheet for your cloth.

Sheets for Round Tablecloths

Diameter of Cloth (Add 1″ for hem)	Flat Sheet Required
Up to 65′	Twin
Up to 80″	Full (Double)
Up to 89″	Queen
Up to 99″	King (Separate Hem)
Up to 107″	King (Self Hem)

ROUND CLOTHS

Round cloths are simple to make, which is a good thing, if you've ever searched for a ready-made cloth larger than 80 inches. Basic round cloths are constructed as follows.

1. Measure the table to determine the required diameter of the cloth. Decide how much drop you wish, noting chair seat height, floor length, and any other considerations. Measure the side drop, the table diameter, and the opposite side drop. Add 1 inch extra to allow for a narrow hem.

2. Fold the fabric in half lengthwise. Then make a square by folding in half again to form quarters. (If your fabric is lightweight you may fold once again to form eighths. However, you may be unable to cut through this thickness on heavier fabrics.)

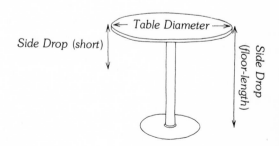

Table Diameter

Side Drop (short)

Side Drop (floor-length)

3. Cut a length of nonstretchy twine to serve as a compass. Attach the cord to the fabric with a corsage pin through a knot. Tie the twine to a pencil or tailor's chalk. Pin the fabric layers together to prevent slipping, if necessary. Mark the outer edge of the cloth with the pencil. (The cord length should be equal to half the desired cloth diameter, plus ½ inch.) Cut and then hem by hand or by machine.

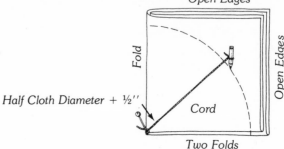

When a cloth must be seamed to create enough width, avoid putting the seam in the center. Instead, make a seam on both sides equidistant from the center. Then follow directions for folding and cutting given in steps 3 and 4. Be sure to allow for a pattern match if your fabric requires it.

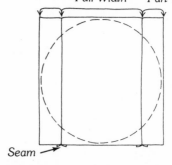

Ideas and Variations for Round Cloths

Short round or square top cloths over floor-length round cloths are practical as well as attractive. Laundering of the large cloth is minimized; small cloths can be rotated with use.

Ruffles in matching or contrasting fabrics are a good way to extend the length of sheets or fabrics not quite wide enough to reach the floor. Hem borders from sheets make quick work of ruffles.

A border of flat cording around a cloth is a custom touch that makes it hang effectively.

Striped fabric seamed in quarters creates a square on the table top and soft draped sides. Eighths create an octagon.

Striped fabric seamed in eighths or quarters with stripes merging in the center creates a starlike design.

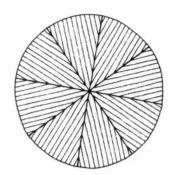

OVAL CLOTHS

Since oval tables vary a great deal in size and shape, the bottom hem of an oval cloth should be marked individually according to the table.

1. Place seamed fabric on the table and center carefully. Weight the cloth with heavy objects around the edge of the table to prevent slipping. Mark the bottom edge of the cloth ½ inch from the floor, or the desired length (including 1 inch for hem) using a hem marker if available, or a folded cardboard gauge. Slide the gauge around the table as needed. Cut the bottom hem edge of the cloth. Machine or hand hem.

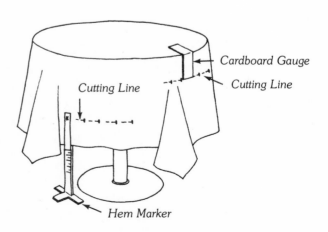

Cardboard Gauge

Cutting Line

Cutting Line

Hem Marker

SQUARE AND RECTANGULAR CLOTHS

As with round and oval cloths, if the fabric must be seamed the pieces should be placed to avoid a seam down the center of the table. Determine the length plus the 2 side drops plus the hem, _____ inches. Determine the width plus the 2 side drops plus the hem, _____ inches.

Table Runners

Table runners combine with long cloths or show off a spectacular glass or wood table to the best advantage. They are easy to make, since they are just long strips of fabric. Why not make them reversible? Then you hem them at the same time you make a second set! Add rick rack, cording, fringe, or appliqués for a custom touch. Runners may be any length or width you prefer. If you plan to use them instead of placemats, they should be at least 18 inches wide.

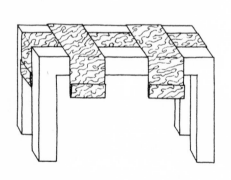
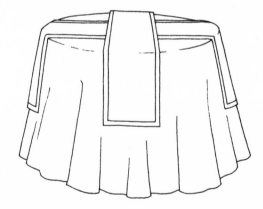

Placemats

Great as gifts or for your own pleasure, placemats can be created in an endless array of sizes, shapes, colors, fabrics, and trims. Look around you for ideas, and put your imagination to work.

BASIC UNLINED MAT

Cut fabric pieces 13 x 19 inches. Turn the hem edges under ¼ inch and press. Then turn them again and stitch by machine or hand. Decorator fabrics often have excellent design motifs that can be centered on a mat or cut out and appliquéd as detail on a plain contrasting fabric.

Quilted fabrics are ideal for placemats. Bind the edges with bias tape or line the mat and turn it to reduce bulk at the hem.

REVERSIBLE PADDED OR QUILTED MAT

1. Cut two pieces of fabric and one piece of polyester fleece 13 x 19 inches for each mat. (Use two coordinated or contrasting fabric prints as desired.) Place the fabric pieces with right sides together. Lay the fleece on top. Pin and stitch with ½-inch seam, leaving a 5- to 6-inch opening for turning.

2. Trim excess fleece from the seam allowances, and trim the corners. Turn and press. To close the opening slip in a narrow piece of fusible web and bond the edges together, or close with hand stitches. Add hand or machine quilting if desired. The fleece pads and opaques, so reversing colors or designs won't conflict with one another.

Napkins

Napkins are a magic way to use up bits and pieces of fabric that are left from other projects. Or when purchasing fabric include an extra yard or two so you'll be sure to have a set of napkins to co-ordinate with your table creations. There is a surprising amount of mileage in a yard or two of fabric.

Cut the fabric to the desired size. Press a ¼-inch hem all around. Turn the hem under ¼ inch more and stitch by machine or slipstitch by hand.

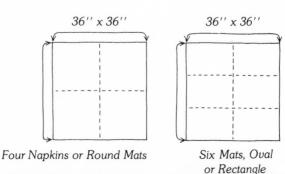

Four Napkins or Round Mats   *Six Mats, Oval
or Rectangle*

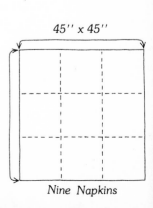

Nine Napkins

Hem Treatments for Table Cloths, Table Runners, Placemats, Napkins

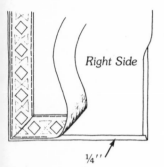

Right Side

¼''

- Use the narrow hemming foot on the machine. This makes a fine rolled and stitched hem.
- Gingham, homespun, and linenlike fabrics can often be self-fringed. Stitch ½ inch from the edges of the fabric with a short stitch length. Using a needle or pin, work the threads loose and unravel them up to the stitching line. Be sure the fabric is cut on grain to assure an even fringe.
- Enclose the raw edge by turning ¼ inch to the right side of fabric. Fuse or stitch a row of trim in place over the raw edge.
- Make smooth mitered corners. First finish the edges by turning them under ¼ inch and machine edge stitching. Then locate the hem depth along each edge. Fold and press the corner on a diagonal at the point where the hem depth lines meet. Refold with the right sides together and stitch on the crease line. Trim the seam allowance. Turn and press the miter. Hem by machine or hand with fusible webbing.

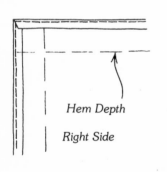

Hem Depth

Right Side

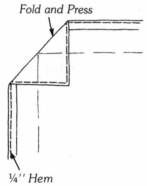

Fold and Press

¼'' *Hem*

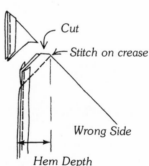

Cut

Stitch on crease

Wrong Side

Hem Depth

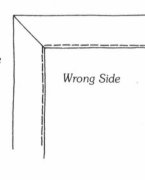

Wrong Side

SIX

FABRICS FOR BED AND BATH

Bedspreads

A bedspread is perhaps the single most important item in a bedroom's decorating scheme. You may plan it to blend with fabric on the walls, or to contrast for heightened emphasis. Since bedspreads are constructed basically of straight seams, they are quite simple to make.

Nearly any fabric may be used for a spread, but its durability should be considered, especially if the bed is used by a child or will double as a day bed or couch. The different bedspread styles will adapt to any fabric from chintz and gingham to velveteen, corduroy, and quilted fabric. Flounced styles work best in sheers and lightweight fabrics, while the throw-style and box-style spreads combine best with medium and heavier fabrics. If you choose a lightweight fabric for a throw-type spread, be sure to consider lining or quilting it for added body. If desired, you can use a lining that creates a reversible spread. Decorator sheets mean fewer, if any, seams in a bedspread.

THROW-STYLE BEDSPREAD

This is a simple flat spread that lends itself well to most decorative schemes. If you must piece fabrics to achieve the needed width, place a full-width panel in the center, piecing on side sections to balance the look. Always avoid a center seam. Corners are often rounded at the foot to keep excess fabric off the floor.

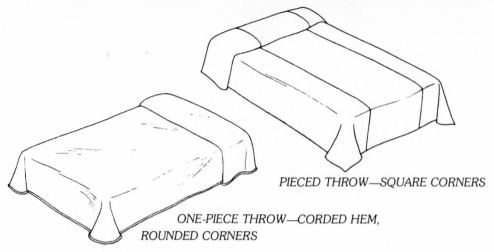

PIECED THROW—SQUARE CORNERS

ONE-PIECE THROW—CORDED HEM,
ROUNDED CORNERS

Determining Yardage

The bed should be made up with pillows and blankets when you are measuring.

1. Length (A) - Measure from the head over the pillows allowing 14 to 15 inches tuck-in, and down to the foot and to ½ inch from the floor. Add extra for a hem.

2. Width (B) - Measure up, across, and down the bed, ½ inch from the floor on each side. Add extra for hems.

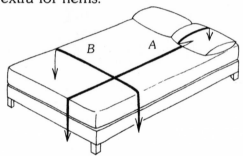

Construction

1. Seam the panels together. Round the corners if you prefer.

2. Hem all the way around, allowing a 2-inch hem at the sides and bottom and a 1-inch hem at the top edge. Use a machine stitched hem or machine blindstitch. Other hem ideas include adding bound bias, braid, or a corded edge.

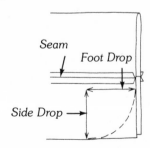

Seam

Foot Drop

Side Drop →

Or if you choose, line the bedspread. The hems will be included in the seams. Only the seam allowances, not the hems, need to be added to the length and width. Prepare the lining as for the spread. Pin the two right sides together. Stitch, and press the seams open. Clip at the corners if necessary. Turn and press the entire spread. Close the top opening. To make edges lie flatter you may wish to topstitch all around the edge of the spread.

BOX-STYLE BEDSPREAD

This is a neatly tailored spread that fits the bed smoothly on all sides. The corners may be box pleats, free underlays, or just slits (best for beds with corner posts). Seams can be accented with cording for a custom touch. Often the top section is lined or quilted for more body. Lining the side pieces is optional. (For lining follow directions for a flounce spread.)

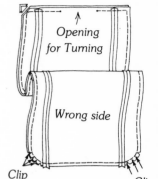

*Opening
for Turning*

Wrong side

Clip   *Clip*

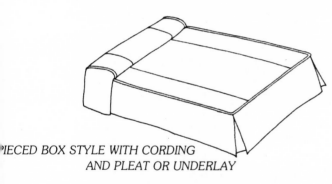

*PIECED BOX STYLE WITH CORDING
AND PLEAT OR UNDERLAY*

*BOX STYLE WITH SLITS
FOR FOOTBOARD*

Determining Yardage

The bed should be made up with pillows and blankets when you are measuring.

1. Top Panel Length (A)—Measure from the head over the pillows, allowing 14 to 15 inches for tuck-in, to the edge of the bed and add 1½ inches for a seam allowance and the top hem.

2. Panel Depth (B)—Measure from the edge of the bed to ½ inch from the floor. Add 2½ inches for a seam allowance and a hem.

3. Top Panel Width (C)—Measure across the bed from edge to edge. Add 1 inch for seam allowances.

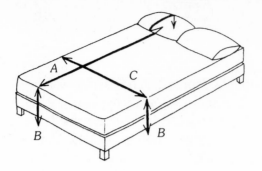

4. The length of the side panels (D) is the length of the three sides of the bed plus hems and allowances for pleats if they are used.

Construction

1. Seam the sections if necessary to create the top panel.

2. Cut and hem the side panel sections according to the corner method to be used. Pin in place and stitch to top panel.

Box Pleats Allow 20 inches for each pleat. Place the seam toward the foot panel on each pleat.

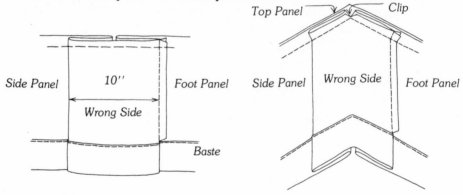

Underlay Cut two sections, each 12 inches wide. Hem the edges and stitch them in place.

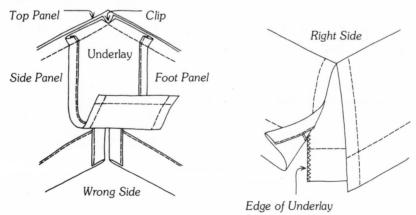

Slits Hem the side panel edges and seam in place so they meet at the corners of the foot of the bed.

Top Panel

Side Panel

Foot Panel

Wrong Side

FLOUNCE BEDSPREAD

This style is softer than others. It is most attractive when constructed of sheer or lightweight fabrics since the gathers become bulky and unattractive when made from heavier fabrics. The spread may be made with slits at the foot to allow for posts in the foot boards. The top section is frequently lined to give added body and stability to the fabric and to conceal the raw edges of the gathered flounce.

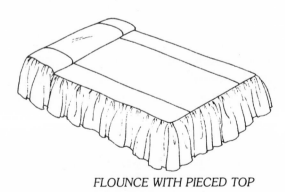

FLOUNCE WITH PIECED TOP

*FLOUNCE WITH SLITS
FOR FOOTBOARD POSTS*

Determining Yardage

1. The top panel length, panel depth, and top panel width are determined as for a box spread.

2. The length of side panels is the length of the three sides of the bed times 2 to 2½ for fullness, plus the hems and seam allowances.

Construction

1. Seam the sections if necessary to create a top panel.

2. Cut, seam, and hem the side panel sections. Mark the top edge with a small clip every 15 inches. Mark the edges of the top panel section in the same way.

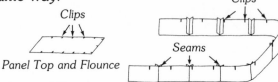

Clips

Clips

Seams

Panel Top and Flounce

3. Gather the top edges of flounce.

● *Method 1*

Place a strong thin cord ⅜ inch from the top edge on the wrong side. Stitch over it with a wide zigzag. Pull the cord to form gathers, adjusting so the clips match the top panel.

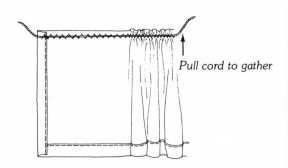

Pull cord to gather

● *Method 2*

Make two rows of machine basting ¼ inch and ½ inch from the raw edge of the flounce. (Buttonhole twist is best since it is strong.) Pull gently on the cords, creating gathers. Adjust the gathers to match the clips on the top panel.

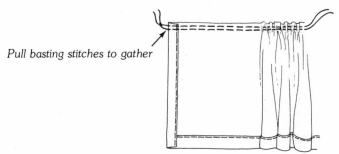

Pull basting stitches to gather

● *Method 3*

Use the gathering foot or ruffler on your sewing machine to gather the flounce.

4. Pin the flounce to the top panel, matching clips to keep the gathers even. Stitch the seam just below the gathering stitches or cord. Overcast the raw edges with a zigzag stitch or bind if desired.

LINING A FLOUNCE OR BOX-STYLE BEDSPREAD

Prepare the lining as for the top section of the spread. Pin the two right sides together with the flounce inside between the two pieces. Stitch the outer edges, taking a few short diagonal stitches across the corners to make them lie smoother. Leave an opening at the top of the bedspread for turning. Trim corners. Press the seams open. Turn and press the entire spread. Close the top opening by hand, machine, or fusible web. If you desire to make the gathers lie smoother, place a line of topstitching around the top near the seamline.

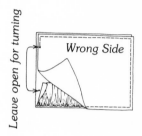

Leave open for turning

Wrong Side

Coverlets

Coverlets are short spreads that end about 3 inches below the mattress and are usually combined with a dust ruffle. They may be made in any of the styles that bedspreads are. Follow the directions for the style of your choice using the bedspread styles, adjusting the yardage and measurements as needed.

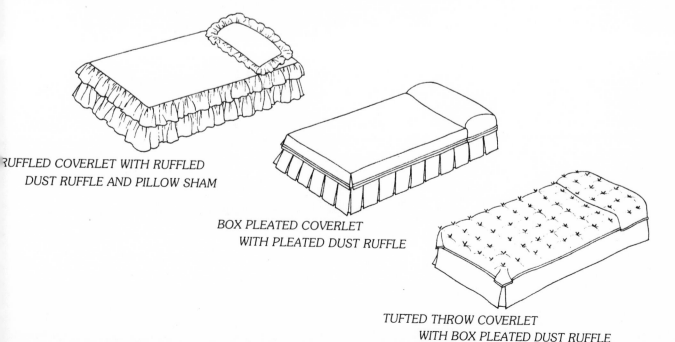

*RUFFLED COVERLET WITH RUFFLED
DUST RUFFLE AND PILLOW SHAM*

*BOX PLEATED COVERLET
WITH PLEATED DUST RUFFLE*

*TUFTED THROW COVERLET
WITH BOX PLEATED DUST RUFFLE*

TUFTED COVERLET OR COMFORTER

A tufted coverlet or full-size comforter is a quick and easy project that can bring a casual softness to any bed. You may also hand-quilt or machine-quilt the coverlet if you prefer. The more layers of quilt batting you use in your comforter, the more size will be taken up in the tying or quilting process, so be sure to allow a few extra inches all around to compensate.

1. Measure as for a throw coverlet or bedspread. Cut and seam the top and bottom pieces to create the necessary width. Round the corners if desired. Lay the top and bottom pieces with right sides together. Anchor them with pins.

2. Lay the quilt batting (available in twin, full, queen, and king sizes, or by the yard, which would need to be pieced) on the wrong side of the top coverlet piece. Pin in place along all the edges and intermittently in the middle as necessary.

3. Stitch around the coverlet, leaving an opening for turning. Trim and clip the corners to reduce bulk and trim the batting close to the stitching line.

4. Turn the coverlet right side out and close the opening by hand or machine. Lay the coverlet out and mark it with pins or chalk at regular intervals, about 10 to 12 inches apart. Thread a large needle with two strands of washable yarn. Sew through all the layers and knot the yarn ends securely on one side. Clip the ends of the yarns to about ¾ inch.

The pattern formed by the ties may be squares, diamonds, or a pattern determined by the design of the fabric.

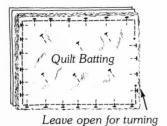

Quilt Batting

Leave open for turning

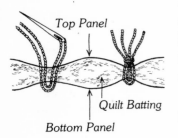

Top Panel

Quilt Batting

Bottom Panel

Dust Ruffles

Dust ruffles are usually flounced and gathered, but they may be tailored with box pleats at the corners, or groups of pleats spaced as desired. They hide the box spring and combine with coverlets for a custom bed treatment. Most fabric types work well for dust ruffles. Sheers and lightweight fabrics look best in gathers, and medium and heavy fabrics are most attractive in smooth, tailored styles.

The ruffle or side strips may be attached to a flat piece of fabric cut to fit the top of the box spring, to a fitted sheet slipped over the box spring, or directly to the edge of the box spring.

Determining Yardage

1. Depth (A)—Measure from the top edge of box spring to the floor. Add 4 inches to allow for the hem, seam allowance, and turn back.

2. Length (B)—Measure the distance around the two sides and foot. Add 1 inch for each seam needed to combine strips to achieve measurement B in the diagram.

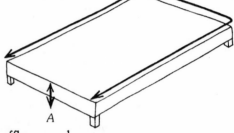

- Double fullness (B X 2) allows for a gathered ruffle or a box-pleated ruffle with 2½-inch-deep pleats 10 inches apart.
- Triple fullness (B X 3) allows for a full gathered ruffle or a box-pleated ruffle with 2½-inch-deep pleats 5 inches apart.

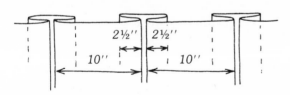

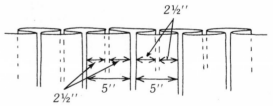

- B + 45 inches allows for a tailored dust ruffle with 5-inch-deep box pleats at the corners of the foot of the bed.

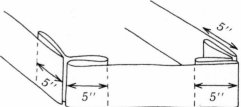

Construction

1. Place a fitted sheet on the box spring. If necessary open the corners at the head of the bed to get the sheet to fit. (Add ties at the open corners to attach the sheet firmly to the bed if necessary.) The sheet should fit snugly and smoothly. (If you prefer, you may cut a piece of fabric or a sheet the same size as the top of the box spring and use this as the dust ruffle base.) Mark the top edge of the box spring every 12 inches on the sides and bottom.

2. Seam the strips of fabric to create the desired finished length as indicated above. Make a narrow hem at the end of each finished strip. Turn up a double hem 1 inch deep at the bottom edge. Stitch or fuse.

3. For a gathered ruffle make short clips every 12 inches along the top edge of the strip.

4. Make two rows of basting stitches along the top edge—one row ¾ inch from the edge, one row 1 inch from the edge. Use a button twist on the bobbin for strength.

• Or stitch double cord shirring tape 1 inch from the top edge. Knot the cords so they won't pull out.

• Or zigzag over a strong fine cord placed 1 inch from the top edge of the fabric.

5. Pull up on the gathering threads or cords. Adjust to fit the marks on the edge of the sheet. Pin the ruffle to the sheet, right sides together, side hems at the head of the bed, edge of the ruffle even with the edge of the box spring. Remove the sheet and ruffle and stitch the ruffle in place 1 inch from the raw edge.

6. Flip the ruffle over into position. Stitch it again next to the seam to hold the gathers in place.

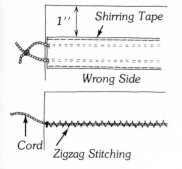

1"   *Shirring Tape*

Wrong Side

Cord   *Zigzag Stitching*

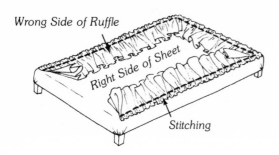

Wrong Side of Ruffle

Right Side of Sheet

Stitching

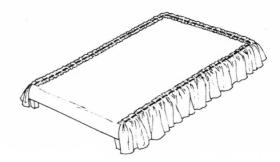

For pleated styles follow the preceding directions. When pinning the strip to the base fabric, start with a pleat at the center
bottom and pin the pleats in place, working around to the head of
the bed, making any small adjustments necessary to allow the
pleats to fall at the corners of the foot. For tailored box style
follow the preceding directions, placing a box pleat 5 inches deep
at each corner of the foot of the bed.

Pillow Shams

Pillow shams are often combined with coverlets and comforters to
reduce the bulk at the head of the bed. If you plan to coordinate
them with a bedspread, you can reduce the length of the spread
about about 14 to 15 inches, the length of the tuck-in.

Shams are loose-fitting covers, often with ruffled, pleated, or
eyelet borders. A lapped opening across the back allows the pillow to be slipped in and out easily.

1. Cut the front section in one piece. Cut the back sections in
two pieces allowing 4 inches additional fabric on each piece to
form an overlay. Make a 1½-inch hem on each piece, then overlap and pin sections so they fit the front section.

2. Pin the ruffle to the right side of the top pillow section, ad-
justing the fullness at the corners. Lay the bottom section in place.
Pin and stitch with a ½-inch seam allowance. Trim the corners.
Turn the sham right side out through the overlap. Press.

Headboards

Take your staple gun or sewing machine in hand and in a short time you will have a padded headboard to coordinate with your new bedspread or coverlet. Firmly woven fabrics work best for these projects. With decorator sheets you will eliminate the need for seams.

PADDED HEADBOARD

Turn a piece of ¾-inch plywood or an old headboard into instant decorating.

1. Wrap and staple the headboard with several layers of quilt batting or a layer of polyfoam with one or two layers of quilt batting over it. Center fabric on headboard and staple along the lower front edge.

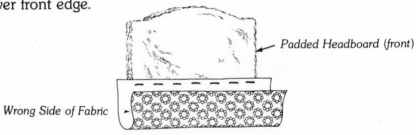

Padded Headboard *(front)*

Wrong Side of Fabric

2. Pull the fabric up and over the headboard. Staple it in place, starting at the center and working toward the sides, alternating back and forth from side to side and keeping the fabric taut and straight.
3. Finish the back by tacking a piece of muslin in place covering raw edges.

HANGING HEADBOARD

Here's a quick economical headboard that hangs on the wall like a picture. Simply push the bed up against the headboard to create a finished look.

1. Cut a piece of ½-inch plywood or Upson board® to the desired size and shape. Cut three or more layers of quilt batting

or a layer of polyfoam the size of the board plus 2 inches all around. Cut one layer of fabric the size of the board plus 3 inches all around. Place batting and then the board on top of the fabric.

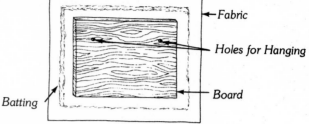

Fabric

Holes for Hanging

Board

Batting

2. Staple batting, then fabric, snugly to board, mitering or pulling the corners in a rounded fashion as desired. To hang, use picture hangers or drill two holes through the board (before wrapping) and hang on two screws anchored to wall studs.

SLIPCOVERED HEADBOARD

1. Wrap the headboard with quilt batting or foam as in step 1 under "Padded Headboard."
2. Cut two pieces of fabric the size of headboard plus ½-inch seam allowances. Cut strips the width of headboard plus ½-inch seam allowances. Be sure to take measurements after the headboard has been padded to assure correct fit of fabric cover. Seam together as shown. Press, clip, and turn right side out. Slip over headboard and tack in place along the bottom or back edge.

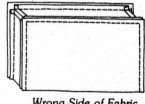

Wrong Side of Fabric

Canopies

Canopies can turn a bed into the focal point of a bedroom. They may be quite simple, or very elaborate depending on decor, fabric, and preference. Here are some easy canopy ideas to consider.

MOUNTING BOARD CANOPY

Staple, starch, or glue fabric to the wall. Then bring it up and over a 1 x 6 inch board covered or painted to match. Trim can be glued or stapled in place to hide the angle irons which hold the board in place. Or wrap and staple the fabric in place after the board has been mounted by bringing it up the wall and under the mounting board.

CURTAIN ROD CANOPY

Mount curtain rod or drapery poles with one on the wall and one suspended or toggle-bolted from the ceiling. Drape fabric up and over the rods to create a canopy effect. Add a shaped or trimmed hem if desired.

STAPLED CANOPY

The simplest canopy is obtained by stapling fabric directly to the wall and out into the ceiling. Trims, fringes, or shaped hems on canopy drop will add a special touch. Just running a panel of fabric to the ceiling is also very effective, even without an overhead canopy.

STAPLED CANOPY

CORNICE AS CANOPY

CORNICE AS CANOPY

A canopy may often be an enlarged cornice or valance. So when searching for canopy ideas for a bedroom, consider cornice techniques, too. See chapter 4 for cornice construction ideas. A cornice over a bed should be at least 12 inches deep and 4 inches wider than the bed if side draperies are to hang from the inside.

CURVED CANOPY

Cover a semicircle of plywood with fabric, then attach it to the ceiling over the bed. Staple a shirred panel behind the bed (or gather onto rods). Staple side drapes to the edges of the plywood, then staple the gathered valance over the top and around the entire edge of the plywood.

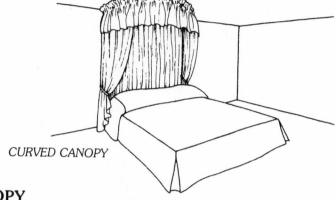

CURVED CANOPY

SLANTED CEILING CANOPY

Take advantage of a slanted ceiling and turn it into a elegant canopy effect. Add side drapes if desired.

CORNER CANOPY

Fabric the walls in the corner the length and width of the bed. Mount a piece of plywood covered with fabric or a wooden fabric-wrapped frame the size of the bed on the ceiling. Staple the side drapes in place to the edge of the frame, then add a ruffle or valance around the entire frame to complete the canopy detail. (Place the side drapes at each corner if desired.)

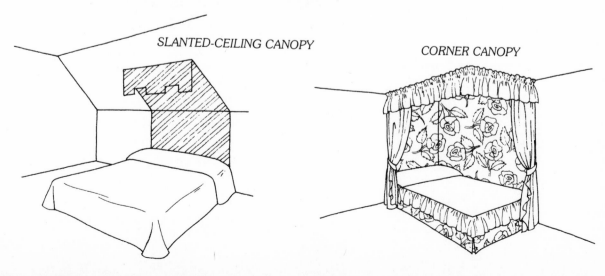

SLANTED-CEILING CANOPY

CORNER CANOPY

Shower Curtains

Ready-made shower curtains can be surprisingly expensive, while making your own is unexpectedly easy. With a plastic liner or old shower curtain beneath, nearly any fabric can be used. A standard shower curtain is usually 6 x 6 feet, so two lengths of 36-inch fabric will work. Wider lengths can be seamed and trimmed to 6 feet or left wider for more fullness. If you like the look of a floor-length curtain, measure and cut accordingly. A center seam is acceptable, although many people prefer to use a full width center panel with narrower side panels as for tablecloths and bedspreads. Using the liner as a pattern and making the finished curtain 1 inch larger all around is a simple way to be sure everything will fit.

1. Cut fabric into 81-inch lengths (unless you are making a floor-length or ceiling-to-floor curtain, then figure accordingly). Seam the fabric panels together as needed for finished width of about 75–76 inches.

2. Turn down the top edge in a double 1-inch hem. Stitch or fuse (fusing adds more body, which is often desirable). Turn a double 3-inch hem at the bottom edge. Stitch or fuse. Repeat at side edges with a double ½-inch hem.

3. Apply grommets or large eyelets or make $5/16$-inch machine buttonholes along the top hem edge. Use the liner as a guide for spacing, or space 12 holes evenly along the top of the curtain, starting in about 1½ inches from the side edge and ½ inch down from the top. Lay the curtain and the liner together. Put shower curtain hooks through both. Hang on shower rod.

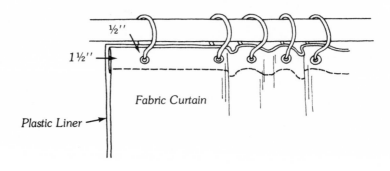

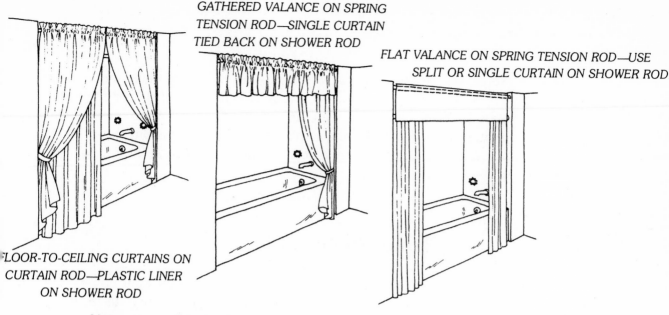

GATHERED VALANCE ON SPRING TENSION ROD—SINGLE CURTAIN TIED BACK ON SHOWER ROD

FLAT VALANCE ON SPRING TENSION ROD—USE SPLIT OR SINGLE CURTAIN ON SHOWER ROD

FLOOR-TO-CEILING CURTAINS ON CURTAIN ROD—PLASTIC LINER ON SHOWER ROD

Valances and tie backs can be used to create additional flair for your bathroom.

FLAT VALANCE

This is one of my favorites because it gives a built-in look to the bath area, hides the shower curtain rod, and still allows air flow for ventilation around the shower area.

1. Make a fabric piece wide enough to fit the bath opening plus 4 inches and long enough to come below the shower rod by 2 to 3 inches, plus 4 inches. (While I usually make this valance flat for the built-in look, you may add width and gather it if you prefer.) Stitch a 1¾-inch casing on the top edge, 1-inch double side hems, and a double 2-inch bottom hem.

2. Install a curtain rod or use a spring tension rod to hold the valance ½ inch from the ceiling. Position the valance on the rod and hang the shower curtain from regular shower rod.

SHORT VALANCE

This style trims the top of the curtain, but does not hide the rod. It is often combined with ornamental shower curtain hooks. A short valance is made to the same dimensions as the shower curtain except that it is 10 to 12 inches long. It is hung with the liner and curtain—the grommets are spaced the same.

Note: Try starching fabric to the outside of sliding glass shower doors. If the doors do not get undue splattering you should have good success. Be sure to wipe up any excess starch from the aluminum frame so that there is no danger of pitting from the salt present in some brands of starch. Try a flat valance at the top for a built-in look.

Toilet Accessories

Standard toilet accessories include a tank lid cover, tank cover, and seat cover. Most ready-mades are from plush or fake-fur fabrics. Sometimes the fabric is so thick that the lid won't stay up without falling over. It is much more exciting to create your own accessories from any fabric—cotton chintz, gingham, velvet upholstery fabric, terry cloth, or towels, sheets, and so on. You can pad them softly for body with polyester fleece or quilt batting, but they won't be thick, and the lid will stay up.

One of my favorite starch tricks is in our bathroom where I made fleece-padded tank lid and toilet seat covers, but starched the 100 percent cotton chintz directly to the toilet tank. Yes, it gets damp from some sweating, but it still holds and it has been there over three years now. I just wash it off occasionally with a sponge. Try it. You've nothing to lose but a small piece of fabric. Some blends may work, but you have to try it to find out for sure.

TANK LID COVER

1. Cut a rectangle of fabric and polyester fleece or quilt batting the size of the lid plus 2½ inches longer and wider. Pin-fit the fabric to the lid with wrong side of fabric up. Sew along pinned lines, trim darts, and press open. Cut away excess padding close to stitching lines.

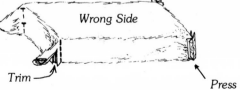

Wrong Side

Trim—

Press open

2. To make the casing, open out one folded edge of the bias fold tape. Pin the tape to the lid cover with the right sides together and the raw edges even. Stitch with ¼-inch seam.

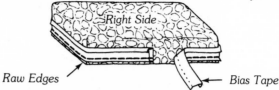

Raw Edges   *Bias Tape*

Right Side

3. Turn the bias to the inside and press. Stitch the folded edge of the bias to the cover, leaving an opening to insert the elastic.

4. Cut a piece of elastic 45 inches long. Pin a safety pin to the end for threading, and one large pin across the other end crosswise. Pull the elastic through the casing. Overlap the ends of the elastic and stitch them together securely.

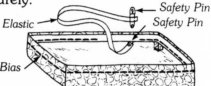

Elastic   *Safety Pin*   *Safety Pin*

Bias

TOILET SEAT COVER

1. Make a pattern by taping a piece of paper to the back of the seat and drawing around it. Add 1½ to 2 inches around the curved edge and 1 inch across the flat bottom edge.

2. Cut a piece of polyester fleece or quilt batting and a piece of fabric according to the pattern and stitch them together at their outer edges.

3. Make the casing by opening out one folded edge of the ½-inch single-fold bias tape. With the right sides together pin the bias to the outer edge of the cover with the raw edges even, curving to fit.

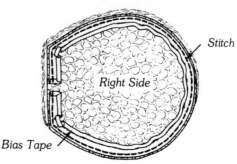

Stitch

Right Side

Bias Tape

4. Turn the tape to the wrong side and stitch it in place, close to the fold.

5. Cut a piece of ¼-inch elastic 32 inches long. Pin a safety pin on one end for threading and crosswise on the other end. Thread the elastic through the casing. Overlap the ends of the elastic and stitch them securely.

TANK COVER

1. Measure around the tank perimeter plus 6 inches. Measure the height of the tank plus 3 inches.

2. Cut the fabric and a layer of padding. Pin-fit darts at the top and bottom. Stitch and trim. Press open. Zigzag or turn under the back edges.

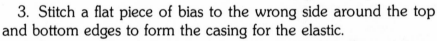

Trim   *Press open*

Pin

Padding

3. Stitch a flat piece of bias to the wrong side around the top and bottom edges to form the casing for the elastic.

4. Cut two pieces of elastic each 36 inches long. Thread them through the top and bottom casings as shown. Overlap the ends of the elastic and stitch them securely.

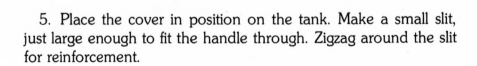

Elastic

Bias Tape

Padding

5. Place the cover in position on the tank. Make a small slit, just large enough to fit the handle through. Zigzag around the slit for reinforcement.

TISSUE BOX COVERS

Fitted and Sewn

1. Cut two pieces of fabric 3 inches longer than measurement A and 2 inches longer than measurement B.

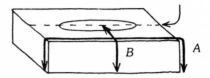

2. Stitch the pieces of fabric right sides together with a ½-inch seam, leaving an opening as long as the opening on a tissue box.

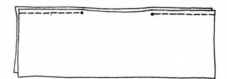

3. Stitch or fuse the seam allowances down. If desired, add trim to the top edges of the opening.

4. Pin-fit, mitering the corners. Stitch, then trim the excess at the corners. Turn the raw edge under ⅜ inch, and stitch it to form the casing for the drawstring or elastic.

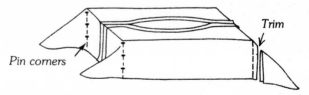

Pin corners   *Trim*

5. Fit the cover over the tissue box. Run a piece of elastic through the casing, drawing it up to fit. Cut and stitch the ends securely.

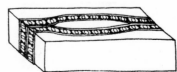

Fused Tissue Box Cover

The simple way to cover a tissue box is to use fusible webbing and bond the fabric directly to the box. If you want to create a re-usable box, first slip a dinner knife or letter opener under the glued flaps on one side or end of the box to open them up. Fuse the fabric to the box, wrapping it around the flaps at least ½ inch. Add nylon fastener tape strips to hold the bottom closed.

Bathroom Organizer

An easy-to-make hanging organizer can give you storage where you need it most and can be an interesting accessory as well. Shelves may be spaced equally or in an uneven pattern to provide space for specific items.

1. Cut three to six 12 x 16 inch shelves from ½-inch plywood or have them cut at a lumberyard. Stain, paint, or wrap the shelves with fabric.

2. Cut two pieces of sturdy fabric 13 inches wide by 12 feet long. Or if you prefer to seam two 6-foot pieces to create each strip, double stitch or flat fell the seams for strength. (You can get four 6-foot strips from two yards of 54-inch fabric.)

For more body and strength, press on an iron-on interfacing strip before stitching, or slip a fusible web layer in to bond the two layers together after strip is stitched and turned. Stitch the three sides with a ½-inch seam allowance. Trim corners and press the seams open. Turn and top press. Turn the ends in and close with stitching or fusing.

3. Fold the strip in half and double stitch a 1¾-inch casing.

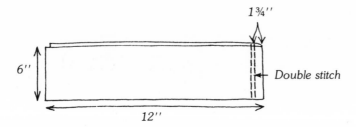

4. Measure 18 inches from the casing stitching and lightly mark a line on each fabric strip (on the inside). Determine the placement of the remaining shelves. Using plain or fancy upholsterer's tacks, tack into the edge of the shelves at about 1- or 2-inch intervals. For bottom shelf, turn the fabric back ¾ inch over a strip of upholsterer's tape and back through tape and fabric to make a strong smooth finished edge.

5. Drill ⁵⁄₁₆-inch holes through a 15-inch length of 1-inch wood dowel ½ inch from the ends of the dowel. Thread a length of nylon rope through the holes and knot the ends to secure them. (The length of the rope determines how far the unit hangs from the ceiling.)

6. Hang your finished unit. Add bath accessories, towels, plants, or magazines.

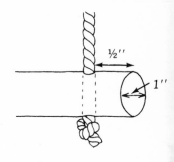

BATHROOM ORGANIZER

Additional Bath Ideas

- Covered wastebaskets, gathered or plain are a nice finishing touch to your decor.
- Stitch bands of fabric to your towels to coordinate them with your decor.
- Make a rug from washable fake fur. Brush on a rubber latex from a carpet or hooked rug store to prevent skidding.

 UICK AND PORTABLE

You have probably at some point found yourself looking for quick and easy decorating ideas to perk up an all-beige apartment, to maintain your budget, to recycle as much as possible, and to keep your landlord happy. Does it sound impossible? This chapter is devoted to helping you realize that many fabric decorating techniques in the preceding chapters can do just that. Of course you'll find lots of other ideas throughout the book, such as light-weight cornices, stretcher bar art, free hanging roller shades, fabric shower curtains, and bath organizer. Use your imagination and get started right away.

Create a Sofa

Create a sofa from a single bed and padded and fabric-covered headboards on each end. Use pillows to fill the back.

Or put two bookcases at each end of the bed with pillows all across the back.

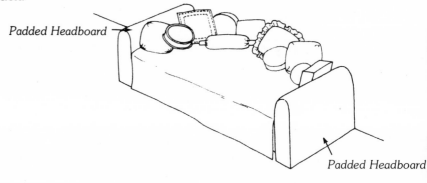

Padded Headboard

Padded Headboard

Napkin Pillows and Placemat Art

A set of batik napkins and placemats can spell excitement at a price you can afford. Use napkins and mats for pillow fronts, using a plain coordinating fabric for the back. Frame placemats on stretcher bars or in chrome gallery frames and group them over the sofa. (Try decorator pillowcases for pillows and wall art, too.)

Drawstring Covers for Worn or Soiled Chair or Sofa Cushions

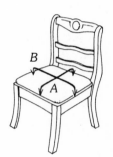

1. Measure the sides and the depth of the chair seat (A) and add 8 inches.
2. Measures the sides and the width of the chair seat (B) and add 8 inches.
3. Round the corners of the fabric piece, then turn under a ½-inch casing all around.
4. Stitch, leaving an opening to run a cord through. Cut the cord the length of the perimeter of the casing plus 12 inches.
5. Center the cover on the cushion and pull the cord. Tie the cord.

Bands of Ribbon, Trim, or Fringe

Tired of dull accessories? Baste or glue trims to make basic beige curtains, drapes, roller shades, lampshades, cornice or venetian blinds coordinate with or perk up your decor. They're easy to

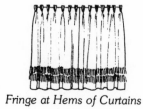
Fringe at Hems of Curtains

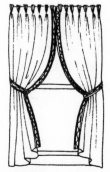
Tiebacks and Centers

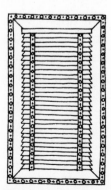
Venetian Blind Tapes

remove, so you can take them with you when you move, or put on new ones when you want another change. Accent venetian blinds—starch trim to frame or wall. Add a touch of trim to a cornice or add a lightweight cornice, then decorate.

Tray Slings

Tray slings made of braid trims and wooden rings also can be used to store and display magazines, toys, sports equipment, and so on. Use several for a planned grouping of objects. Vary the length of the braid according to object to be held.

1. For an 18-inch-long sling sew the ends of a 2-yard piece of 2-inch-wide trim securely by folding the raw ends under and stitching.

2. Thread a loop through the ring with the length divided in half and the seam hidden behind trim.

3. Spread the loops apart where they overlap and stitch them in place.

4. Hang the sling on the wall and insert the object you wish to display.

Hideaways or Extra Storage

Round end, bedside, or dining tables appear from nowhere when you apply a round of plywood over an old console TV set, unfinished bookcase, bedside stand, or packing crate. (The latter also supply extra hidden storage.) Cover the table with a round floor-length cloth and there it is.

Decals and Borders

Decals and border trims can be cut from fabrics and applied to walls, woodwork, cabinets, lamp bases, refrigerators, or just about anything. The simplest way to apply decals or short lengths of border is to pour liquid starch into a flat pan, dip the fabric into the starch to saturate thoroughly, remove excess, then smooth the fabric onto the wall, picking up any drips or runs with a sponge. Starch bands of ribbon trim to fit a flat area on window, door, or picture frame molding. (Ribbons have neat nonraveling edges.) This is a nice touch with windows that have roller shades or venetian blinds.

Slipovers

Flat runner slipovers can be used to hide and disguise old worn furnishings, or simply help them fit into a new decorating scheme. Slipovers may be made of a terrific print or a textured fabric trimmed with braid or fringes. Be sure to double the fabric if the runner will be visible from both sides.

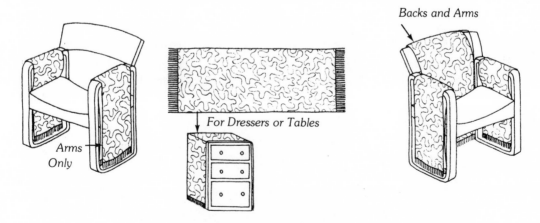

Backs and Arms

Arms Only

For Dressers or Tables

Crossed Flat Runners for Cubes, Card Tables, Parsons Tables

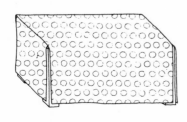

Director's Chair Covers

The easiest way to make a director's chair cover is to use the old one for a pattern. Unless you are making a new cover from the same type and weight of sturdy canvas, the best method is to attach a new cover to the old one so that it serves as support to the new lighter weight fabric. Knit-back fake fur fabrics and suedelike fabrics also need this support.

1. Slip the back off the chair and wrap it with new fabric, turning the top and bottom edges under and overlapping and double stitching the new cover through the same stitching line as the original cover.

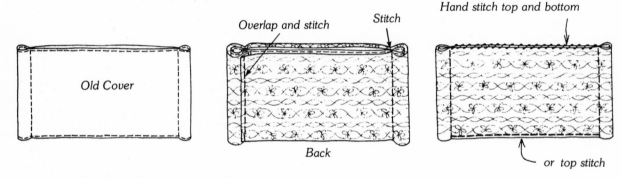

Old Cover

Overlap and stitch

Stitch

Back

Hand stitch top and bottom

or top stitch

2. Remove the seat from the chair. Wrap the new fabric over the seat only. Do not cover the area near the dowels as this makes the fabric too thick to slide back into the channels in the chair frame.

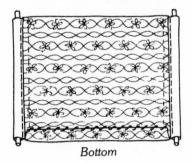

Bottom

SLIPCOVERED BACK AND PILLOW SEAT

A corded seat cushion and a slipcovered back made from quilted fabric (purchased or made) makes a comfortable and unusual director's chair accent.

1. Pin-fit quilted fabric to the chair back over the frame, with wrong sides of the fabric together. Draw in a stitching line with pencil or tailor's chalk. Trim off any extra fabric, leaving about a ¾-inch seam allowance. Baste the seam, turn right side out, and check for fit. The cover should fit smoothly and snugly without pulling. Add cording if desired, then stitch the seams permanently. If cording is not used, turn under the bottom edges or bind them with bias or braid. Slip the cover over the chair back.

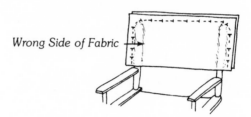

Wrong Side of Fabric

2. Make a corded knife-edge pillow with rounded corners (see chapter 5) to fit the chair seat between the wooden rails. (Make it a tie-on if you wish.)

Side Detail

Slip-Covered Back and Pillow Seat

Tie-Ons

Simple pillows that tie onto a chairseat, chair back, bench, pillow, or headboard are easy accents to take with you when you move. Generally, they are knife-edge pillows (plain, corded, or ruffled) cut to fit the area to be covered. Ties are included in the seams before the pillow is stitched and turned. Ties may be added at two or at all four corners, and along the edges where necessary. The placement and length of ties must be planned for each individual project.

Sono Tube Furniture

Sono tube is the common name for cardboard forms that are used to make concrete structures like steps and pillars in the building industry. You can find them at concrete companies and building construction suppliers. These waxed cardboard forms come in diameters from 4 inches to 48 inches. As the diameter increases so does the thickness and the strength of the tube. Sono tubes are usually sold by the foot, sometimes with a cutting charge. They provide endless possibilities for an imaginative do-it-yourselfer.

PLANT STANDS

SONO TUBE

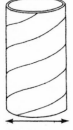

8'' diameter

Use 8- or 10-inch sono tubing. Cut it about 3 feet long (or any length you prefer). Cover it with fabric or Mylar™ (see hardware), add a plastic pot for a liner, then set in your favorite plant or fern. Grouping several planters of various heights in a corner creates a great focal point for a room.

Sono tubes of other diameters can form the base for:
• Stools, tables
• Wastebaskets
• Lamps

Fabric Glued or Stapled to Tube

- Baseball bat racks
- Umbrella stands
- Toy boxes
- Children's toys

Planter

Up light

Table Base

Umbrella Stand

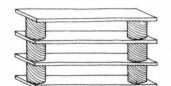

Stretched Wall Art

Hanging Shelf

Tube-and-Board Bookcase

Wall Organizer

Extra portable storage for kitchen, office, child's room, laundry, closet door, or bath can be achieved by stitching pockets of various sizes to a sturdy backing that can be hung on rods. If you choose a lighter weight fabric, fuse two layers of it together with fusible web to add stability and body. Then bind or trim the raw edges with braid or bias.

Hardware

Angle Iron   An L-shaped bar of metal used for joining two pieces of wood or metal. For example: joining cornice to wall, mounting board to window frame.
Awl   A sharp-pointed tool used for starting holes before screw or nail is inserted.
Awning Cleat   Small device attached to side of window frame. Used to secure cords for Roman shades, Austrian, or bamboo shades.
Bi-Fold (*Double-Acting*) *Hinge.* Permits doors or folding screens to swing in both directions.
Brass Weight Rod   Solid metal rod used for added weight and stability for Roman shades and Austrian shades.
Chair Glides   Metal or nylon buttons which can be pounded into the bottom of a chair leg, table leg, or folding screen. Protects floors, allows objects to slide easier, and protects the fabric.
Corrugated Fastener   (wiggle-tail). Small grooved metal strip used to form joints as in screens and window frames, or to tighten loose joints.
Hollow Wall Fasteners   Special screws used when it is necessary to drive into a wall where there are no studs. Here are three examples: *Plastic Expansion Anchors* For medium-weight articles like small shelves, drapery hardware, soap dishes. Plastic sleeve is tapped into hole in wall. As the screw goes in, the sleeve spreads to grip the wall. Get size long enough to pass through wall. If the sleeve is too short, it won't work.

  Molly Screw Anchor   Stronger than above. Slips through hole and fans out and up to grip wall as it is screwed in. Molly is set if screw begins to turn hard and if flange under screw head begins to turn with the screw.

  Toggle Bolts   Strongest of all. Used for really heavy things. Small-size toggle can be used when other methods won't hold. Wings open out after they are pushed through the hole, and open and spread as bolt is tightened.

Molding Hooks   Curved hooks which fit on wood picture molding around top of ceiling in older homes. Can be used to hang pictures, cornices, or fabric while you are applying it to the wall.

Nails   classed according to size and shape. Holding power depends on density of wood and type of nail.

Picture Hangers   This type of hanger may be used to hang cornices as well as pictures. Available in a range of sizes to hold a variety of weights on the wall.

Plumb Bob   A weight attached to the end of a line. Line is rubbed with chalk and then snapped against the wall to mark true vertical. Useful in applying fabric to walls.

Screw Eye/Screw Hook   For hanging and anchoring objects. Available in a wide range of sizes and strengths.

Screen Staples   U-shaped sharp-pointed staples available in many sizes. May be used in cornice techniques.

Square   Metal L-shaped ruler, used to determine if edges are "true" and for perfect 90° angles. Use for stretcher bars, roller shades, folding screens, curtains, drapes.

Staple Gun   Device which shoots staples with pressure and force. Used extensively to apply fabric to walls, screens, chairs, and other surfaces. Also available in electric models.

Wood Joiners   Same uses as corrugated fasteners. These sharp-toothed clips hold two pieces of wood securely, and are easy to pound into the wood.

Lumber

Dowels   Round wood lengths. Available in diameters from ⅛'' to several inches. Used in Roman shade, wall hanging, and other accessory construction.

Fiberboard   A soft, fibrous compressed board also known as *bulletin board*.

Furring Strips   Thin wood strips attached to wall when the surface is rough or uneven. Fabric or paneling is then attached to the furring strips.

Half Round Molding   Wood lengths which have been finished with a flat side and rounded side. Can be used to trim edges of fabric on ceilings and walls, or in shirred fabric wall methods. Also in quarter round and other shapes.

Homosote®   A strong fiber or composition board. Light, inexpensive, easy to use. Ideal for cornices and covered panels.

Upson Board®   Cardboard composition board. Can be sawed easily into shapes. Use for cornices and other wall treatments. From lumber supply in ⅛'', ¼'', ³/₁₆'', and ½''.

Notions

Austrian Shade Tape   Twill tape with woven shirring cords and pre-spaced plastic rings; used to make Austrian shades.

Buckram   A heavily stiffened fabric or fiber substance. Available in several widths, it can be used in cornice construction.

Crinoline   Similar to buckram, but not as stiff. Four-inch strips are used in the construction of drapery headings.

Eyelets and Grommets   Circular reinforcements for holes in fabric. Sizes range from ⅛″ to an inch or more. Smaller types are applied with a special plier; larger ones are usually pounded into place. Used on Roman shades and shower curtains as well as other accessory items.

Fusible Web   Meltable webs of synthetic fibers. Placed between objects, heated with an iron, they melt and fuse the materials together. Washable and dry cleanable. Available in strips or 18″ widths by the yard.

Hook and Eye Tape   Two fabric strips, one containing metal hooks, the other metal eyes. Used to join two strips of fabric as in cornices or dust ruffles, etc. Available by the yard. Should be pre-shrunk.

Hot Iron Cleaner   Available in tubes. A waxy substance used to remove dirt and residues such as fusible web from the soleplate of a hot iron.

Nylon Fastener Tape   A stiff tape with hooks on one side and a very fuzzy surface on the other. When pressed together the bond is very strong, but can be peeled apart easily.

Pleater Tape   A 4″-wide fabric tape with woven in pockets. Tape is stitched to a drapery or curtain heading, then hooks are inserted into pockets to form pinch pleats.

Polyester Fleece   Washable, cleanable ⅛″-thick polyester batting of closely compressed random fibers. Excellent for padding and opaquing. Available by the yard.

Push Pins   Plastic-headed pins useful for holding fabric in place on cornices, walls, stretcher bars, chair seats, etc. while you are positioning and adjusting it for stapling or starching or glueing.

Quilt Batting   A less opaque and thicker batt of polyester than fleece. Used in the construction of quilts or quilted fabrics, and can be used as a stuffing or padding for other projects. Available in bed sizes (twin, full, queen, king) or by the yard.

Roman Shade Tape   Cotton twill tape with plastic rings sewn to tape at intervals. Tape is sewn to fabric, then threaded with cord to form pleats when cord is pulled.

Shirring Tape   A woven tape with heavier cords woven into the construction. Sew flat to fabric, pull up cords and fabric gathers automatically. Available by the yard in 2-cord and 4-cord styles.

Snap Tape   Fabric tape with snaps attached at regular intervals. Available by the yard or in shorter pre-packaged lengths. Should be pre-shrunk.

Twill Tape   A non-stretchy cotton or polyester tape available by the yard in width from ¼″ to over an inch wide. Very strong. Can be used for binding edges or for reinforcement on the back of shades.

Art and Miscellaneous Supplies

Foamboard Smooth tag-board with layer of lightweight foam in the middle. Strong and light. Easily cut into intricate shapes. Available at art supply and display stores in ¼'', ½'', and 1'' thick sheets in sizes 4' x 8' and smaller.

Glue *White craft glues* dry faster and more flexible than all-purpose white glues usually found in the home. Excellent for applying trims to roller and lampshades as well as other accessories.

> *Laminating Adhesive* Available by the quart or gallon through roller shade shops and drapery departments. Dries flexible, clear, and fast. Worth the trouble to find.

> *Spray Adhesive* Aerosol adhesives are found in art supply departments. Excellent for smaller projects, available in many brands and types.

> *Mylar*™ A shiny silver, gold, or copper-colored film available in 54'' widths from art supply or display stores. The vinyl-backed variety is stronger and more flexible. Use for walls, plant stands, shelves, etc., for a mirror or chrome effect.

Upholsterer's Tape Narrow cardboard tape available in strips or rolls from upholstery supply. Used for sharp edges and seams.